THE BURDEN
OF FREEDOM

THE BURDEN
OF FREEDOM

Americans and the
God of Israel

PAUL M. VAN BUREN

A CROSSROAD BOOK
The Seabury Press, New York

The Seabury Press
815 Second Avenue, New York, N.Y. 10017

Copyright © 1976 by The Seabury Press, Inc.

Printed in the United States of America

LIBRARY OF CONGRESS CATALOGING IN PUBLICATION DATA

Van Buren, Paul Matthews, 1924–
The burden of freedom.

"A Crossroad book."
1. Freedom (Theology)—Addresses, essays, lectures.
2. Judaism—United States—Addresses, essays, lectures.
I. Title.
BT810.2.V36   230   76–15181   ISBN 0–8164–0318–X

CONTENTS

PREFACE

Several things should be said before we begin. This little book consists substantially of a revision of a series of lectures given at Holy Cross Abbey, Canon City, Colorado, in August, 1975, where I had been invited to address myself to the theme, "Freedom as a Christian Goal." It deals with extremely large and complex issues in rather few pages and in as simple and direct a manner as the author can manage. The consequence, of which the reader should be as aware as the author, is that only a few of the many aspects of these issues have been brought into focus and only a few of the many possible avenues leading out from them have been explored. There is much more that needs to be said on these matters, and when present administrative duties are set aside, I hope to take up these questions on a scale more befitting their importance.

Second, a word of explanation is perhaps due to any reader who may become puzzled while reading, by recalling the association of the author's name with the so-called Death-of-God Theology of a dozen years ago. That association, it should be noted, was made by others, not by the author, on the basis of their own reading of his *The Secular Meaning of the Gospel* (1963). In *Theological Explorations* (1968) and *The Edges of Language* (1972), a path from that earlier book to this little one may be discerned, which may clarify how the two can come from the same person. If there is a continuing thread throughout my work as a theologian, it may be, as a friend called it to my attention recently, a continuing quest for the concrete. From *The Secular Meaning of the Gospel* through what follows, my concern has been to keep theology's feet on the ground.

Biblical quotations are from the Revised Standard Version, except where I have occasionally made my own translations.

Finally, I should like to take this opportunity to express my sincere appreciation to Sharon Ramey, Secretary to the Department of Religion at Temple University. There is at least no mystery about the freedom which I have had to do the reading, thinking and writing that led to this book. Had she not shouldered so much of the burden of running the affairs of the department, that freedom would have been quite impossible.

THE BURDEN
OF FREEDOM

INTRODUCTION

During his only visit to the United States, Karl Barth was reported to have expressed the hope that there would arise a theology in this land that would be genuinely American, and that if that were to happen, it would be a theology of freedom. As an American theologian for whom Barth's thought has been a recurring stimulus for more than twenty years, I want to deal with that theme as a challenge to begin rethinking the subject matter of Christian faith in a way that might be particularly helpful for thoughtful Christians in America. I do so with the hope that these observations may make a small contribution to the challenging if difficult enterprise of serious Christian reflection.

The enterprise of theology *hic et nunc* in America is challenging on several levels as well as fraught with difficulties. Barth could hardly have been asking for the production of a theology simply bearing the stamp, "Made in U.S.A." That label has now been spread around the globe, stamped on every bomb, tank, plane and ship that imposes the American will on too many millions starving to death or suffering under American-supported tyranny. Thanks to the CIA and the transnational corporations which the CIA apparently exists to defend, that label has become for most people anything but a mark of freedom. Barth was properly suspicious of America, and since his death, we have had enough "cover-ups" uncovered to know full well the ambiguity of speaking of an American theology of freedom. If there could be such a thing, then it would have to be free also to examine its American origin with the utmost critical care.

There have been, however, two recent developments which lend promise to the project of fresh theological reflection. The first is the growing disenchantment of thoughtful people with the promises and possibilities of western civilization generally, and, especially for American Christians, with the American dream in particular. The cultural religion toward which Christianity has tended becomes a bit easier to identify and to resist as the character and consequences of our way of life and system of political economics comes daily more sharply into focus. The evident failure of America and its allies to offer Southeast Asians any alternative to a Marxist-inspired vision of a new social order has suggested to more and more people that in fact we have no alternative. All we seem to have to offer is a more massive technology, and even we are discovering that only a fraction of the population benefits from that, whereas it constitutes a serious threat to the health of the whole people.

As disenchantment with the American myth spreads, it becomes more possible to entertain the thought of Christianity as a counterculture, rather than as a cultural support of the establishment. The increasingly convincing evidence that the American people have been lied to and are still being lied to by their highest officials is not at first sight a matter of theological import, yet this realization may be of benefit in loosening the stranglehold which the values, standards and canons of western civilization have had upon Christians, especially in this country. The emergence of an increasingly interesting Marxist-Christian dialogue may be a sign of this. So too is the beginnings of attention to the challenge of fellow Christians from the Third World, especially from Latin America, pressing to see whether there are any Christians in North America who will side with them against the interests which control their governments and our own, and determine their policies. A generation ago such matters were called "non-theological factors" in the ecumenical movement. That Christians today are no longer so sure that these factors are non-theological may indicate the beginning of fresh theological reflection.

Before turning to a far more important development bearing on the possibilities for theological renewal in our time, it may be necessary to make clear how I am using the term "theology." The typical American Christian, despite the grand if generally forgotten example of Reinhold Niebuhr, seems on the whole to think of theology as some sort of esoteric hair-splitting carried out by insular academicians in incomprehensible jargon. In its popularized form, theology is taken to be the instruction which experts provide for the uninitiated. That is obviously not what I have in mind when speaking of theology. What I am referring to is simply what any and every Christian does whenever he or she thinks over what to do or say about some immediate matter at hand. When theology is so conceived, it follows that there are no non-theologians in the churches.

There may be plenty of poor theologians and sick theologies, but Christians no more have the option of not being theologians than they have of ceasing to think. If we are human we shall think, so if we are Christians, we shall theologize, for better or worse. In which case, we hardly need *more* theology in America. What we may well need is better theology, more self-conscious, better informed, and more critical theology. By "theology," then, I mean nothing more nor less than critical reflection by Christians about the One whom they believe has set them in this world, and about this world in which he has set them.

There has taken place another development in recent years that is of almost incalculable consequence for Christian reflection and which opens up the reflective task in a new and exciting way and as a special challenge to Christians living in America. I refer to the increasing visibility of Judaism in our time, a heightened sense of Jewish identity among Jews, and a slowly increasing awareness of and respect for Judaism on the part of some Gentiles. The fact that the estimated Jewish population of the United States is more than double that of any other country of the world has made this development a particularly evident challenge for American theology.

The renewal of Judaism in our time, as a historical development having historic consequence for Christian theology, has its beginning, of course, in the birth of the state of Israel. The birth and the survival of this tiny state has been a fact of profound importance for Jews of all persuasions, be they religious or secular, Orthodox or Reformed, whether feeling called to move to Israel or choosing to remain in the Diaspora. Jews as well as others have not been and are not now of one mind about the policies of the Israeli government, but it is difficult to find a Jew who does not feel some sense of identification with Israel or who has no commitment to it at all. The birth and survival of that small country in less than hospitable surroundings has played an incalculable role in strengthening the sense of identity of almost all Jews everywhere, and not least in that land of their largest Diaspora, the United States.

From this strengthening has followed a further development: Jews have begun slowly to speak of the unspeakable, to confront the fact of the Holocaust, that valley of dry bones out of which this exceeding great host has arisen (*cf.* Ezek. 37:1–10). There was nothing inevitable about this further development. On the contrary, it might seem more probable that the silence would have continued. Certainly one would not have expected the Gentiles to open that book. No, if the silence was to be broken, it had to be the Jews who made the first move, although doing so was for them an agonizing, even traumatic experience, like the breaking of a solemn oath. Another people might have succeeded in forgetting the past and looking only to the future, but the Jews are a historical people and it is part of their identity and destiny to remember. So it happened that the memory began to break out in tearful stammers, screams of anguish, and historical analyses, hardly an attractive matter, but unavoidably on the agenda of any who wish to do their thinking in relationship to the facts of twentieth-century history.

Confronted by the facts of Jewish renewal, the existence of the state of Israel, and the Holocaust out of which these came, a few Christians have begun to speak of Judaism in tones markedly different from those which have characterized the first nineteen centuries of the life of the Church. From both Catholics and Protestants, one began to hear voices calling into question the long-sanctioned anti-Judaism of the churches. Increasingly, although the numbers are not yet large, Christians are beginning to speak with a new awareness that Jews are among their hearers, and with a growing awareness that history itself has refuted the historian Toynbee's myth that Judaism is the fossil remnant of a dead civilization. The Jews have of course been there all along. What makes the present situation of theology new and interesting is that at least some Christians have become aware of the fact. Two of the most recent signs of this new awareness and of its invigorating if radical consequences for theology are Rosemary Ruether's *Faith and Fratricide* (1974) and Franklin Littell's *The Crucifixion of the Jews* (1975), which together mark the point of no return for Christians with eyes to see. Christian theology is possibly in for a reconstruction that may eventually make the sixteenth-century Reformation look like a minor ripple in the unbroken story of Christianity before it came face to face with the facts of history.

As a modest contribution to the beginning of this reconstruction, I offer the following reflections on the mysterious burden of freedom. I use the word "mystery" in the title of each of the chapters as a reminder that reconstruction is called for in our whole understanding of the subject matter of Christian faith.[1] If we

---

[1] I prefer to use the word "mystery," rather than "paradox" or "dialectic." This choice is dictated by the fact that the problem is not one of logic or philosophy more generally, but of theology. Paradox occurs when it is held that two mutually contradictory assertions are true. Dialectic, an ancient term for philosophy, has become, since Hegel, a term for the relationship between two concepts or forces of history which so work upon each other

attend to the concrete history in which we live, then much that we have learned about the nature of freedom stands in need of reconstruction. Most of this world's dictatorships, a high proportion of its political prisoners, and no small amount of plain old-fashioned slavery are all to be found in what is called "the Free World." Within the same world, the economic norm is called "free enterprise," a strange term for what could more accurately be called "special-interest socialism," or government by and for major industrial corporations. In that same world, those few who can afford it are free to choose their own doctor, the vast majority being presumably "free" to die without benefit of medical care. With such facts becoming increasingly clear to American Christians, this matter of freedom seems not quite so straightforward as they might like it to be.

Moreover, the living presence of Judaism stands as a concrete question mark to much that Christians have said to each other about the freedom of the Christian and about a redemption already achieved, a salvation already realized. With eyes open to the facts of the past nineteen centuries, and not least to the facts of this twentieth century, how are we to understand the apostle Paul's assertion that "for freedom Christ has set you free" (Gal. 5:1), or that of the Gospel according to John (8:36) that "if the Son makes you free you will be free indeed"? In the face of Judaism's living reminder of the concrete, historical character of Israel's messianic hope,

---

as to produce a synthesis, which in turn becomes the starting point for a further development of the same sort. The movement of thought which shall occupy us in this book, however, is rather that of the startled awakening to a realization that things are other than they seem, that our conceptions of freedom, both God's and man's, are not in need of a corrective but are profoundly wrong and need to be reconstructed in a radically new way.

can we seriously maintain that the liberation of the messianic age has already come upon *us?* If we believe in a living God, not one who is only the God of a distant past, nor one who is only a God of the future, but truly a God here and now, then it ought to be in the light of our present history that we do our thinking and re-thinking as Christians in attempting to come to terms with the mystery of freedom.

1. THE MYSTERY OF GOD'S FREEDOM

Theology is, or arises out of, our reflection as Christians about many things, but the central focus is God. Our reflections on freedom, therefore, will properly begin with the matter of God's freedom. Such a beginning parts company with much of recent theology, in which professional theologians seem to be preoccupied with what they call methodology, but which seems rather to be a preoccupation with themselves. Ourselves as secular, Post-Critical, or rational thinkers is not an unusual starting point. The difficulty with such a beginning is that it seems, all too often, never to lead to serious reflection about God.

I shall begin, rather, by presenting right at the start a thesis concerning God's strange freedom, and devote this first chapter to considering its meaning and the case for maintaining it: *The God of Abraham, Isaac and Israel, the God of Sinai and the God of Jesus Christ is the God of freedom in such a way as to prove his freedom by qualifying it to make room for the freedom of his creatures. He is free to make his freedom dependent on theirs, so that the realization of his freedom awaits the realization of the freedom of the sons and daughters of God.*

He who would speak of God surely intends to speak of the One who is the Giver and, in some way, the Lord of life and of all that is real in this world. He who would speak of God, then, intends to speak of him who is the most real. Yet there is something utterly unreal or impossible about this intention. If it be granted that we are not deceived or deluded in our conviction that God exists, then all the more must we acknowledge that everything we say about God must be absurd, mere creaturely babbling concerning a Creator who is so other, so transcendent to our creaturely visions and imagination, not to speak of our human language and concepts, that our words about him must be deemed worthless. Surely if God is, he is unknowable, and this has been said far more insistently by those who are called "believers" than by any self-styled atheist who ever lived. Skeptical philosophers write essays to show what every believer knows in his heart, that not only can God's existence not be proved by us, we can't even adequately refer to him. Our words may aim at God, so to speak, but if he is even remotely near to what we say of him, then our words are at work on a task as far beyond their powers as a Creator is beyond his creatures. It could not be otherwise if it were indeed God of whom we wished to speak. The Rabbis and Church Fathers, the mystics and the best philosophers of both Judaism and Christianity have known this all along.

That strange, impassioned genius of Vienna, Ludwig Wittgenstein, protesting the mush and slush of verbiage flowing out of that capital of a decaying empire (not unlike what one hears daily coming out of Washington, capital of a degenerating empire today), insisted that what could be said, could be said clearly, and that which we cannot speak of, we must remain silent about. Silence is surely a way worthy of the highest respect. If, nevertheless, we feel compelled to attempt to speak of the unspeakable, we need to remind ourselves repeatedly of the foolishness of our words. There can be no other course for us than to join King David in his naked dance before the ark going up to Jerusalem, "making merry before the Lord" (2 Sam. 6:5, 14, 20–21). Theology can be no more but also no less serious than that.

There can be another, if less important, difficulty in speaking of God. It may be that there are some who feel compelled to speak of him because they have had certain experiences in which they believe they have heard, felt, or become aware of God; but what of those who have had no such experiences? For these, it would seem that they can only speak of God "secondhand," as it were. Perhaps so, but there is also this to be said: a person may sense, acknowledge, or even choose identification with a people and its traditions in which others have spoken of God. A person may come to know oneself as part of a linguistic community in which God is spoken of and thus come to share in the intention of that community to speak of God. This identification might come about by way of birth and by long association. It might come from respect for the persons of such a linguistic community who seemed to express best its way of life, values and practices. However this identification may come about in a particular case, for many, this writer included, the intention to speak of God need not imply, nor result from, nor depend upon any sort of religious experience. It can arise also out of an awareness of one's unity with a people who, seeing the world in a certain way, find themselves driven to speak of God.[1]

Both the Christian and the Jewish communities and traditions have maintained that the God of whom they wish to speak is free. It has even been said by some of the rabbis and some Christian theologians, that God is absolutely free, that he can do whatever he chooses, being without any limitations whatsoever. Is this right? How should we decide what is the proper thing to say about God's freedom? Let us leave to the Jewish people their own way of dealing with this question and reflect on the way in which Christians need to think about this matter.

For Christianity, that is, for Christians, the question of what we should say about God may be answered insofar as we can agree among ourselves that we are a people under orders, and therefore not free to give *any* answer we please. We shall consider ourselves under orders insofar as we can acknowledge that we have a living Lord. If we accept that the Church has a Lord, then we are granting that the Church is under orders and must settle such matters by listening and obeying. This is, I believe, what has been at stake in the assertion that Christianity is a religion of revelation. Believing in a living Lord who speaks, the Church listens attentively to the witnesses to certain events in which it believes

---

[1]William James and Ludwig Wittgenstein have helped me to see that most of what we claim to know and believe we have from others, trusting in their general reliability. So it can be with what we call "faith." One may not have heard "the word of the Lord" oneself nor have "felt his presence," and yet have come to trust certain righteous men and women, who themselves say they have heard or seen what one has not, and who seem to know what life is about and how to live it. In this way, one may come to trust and know him whom he or she does not know.

its Lord has spoken. Those particular interpretations, i.e., the biblical writings, of particular events, namely the history of Israel from the escape from Egypt to Easter, are taken by Christians as a clue to the character of reality, because through these interpretations of these events, Christians down through the centuries have, again and again, heard their master's voice speaking to them. Not every religion is a religion of revelation. Taoism, Buddhism, Transcendental Meditation and the Way of Gurdjieff are examples of religions which hold to interpretations of reality that do not depend upon interpretation of historical events. Not so Judaism and Christianity, those two crippled children, as I shall argue, of the one history of God's Israel. They are both rooted in a particular history and its particular interpretation, and that is what is at the heart of their designation as religions of revelation.

The issue, however, is not focused on certain events in the past, although questions about those events and the biblical interpretations of them are unavoidable and vital for Christian faith. Revelation is not primarily a matter of the past but of the present. A religion of revelation, if it is living trust in a living God, and not simply a musty museum of interesting antiquities, is a religion in which it is claimed that the word of a Lord, of a Boss, may be heard *now* through those biblical interpretations. It is a faith for which Jesus's words to his disciples, "He who hears you hears me," are actually fulfilled. When that hearing takes place, then we have a religion of revelation; we have orders rather than speculation, a voice to listen to in answer to the question, "What does it mean to say that our God is the God of freedom?"

One last point before we listen to our orders: when

we make final appeal to what we hear today in the interpretation of apostles and prophets of the events from Sinai to Golgotha, we must thereby admit that we have but one defense, but one justification for the attention which we give to those events and that interpretation. If we could turn to some other court of final appeal, or if we had any other warrants for listening to them, then this other court and these other warrants would be our source of revelation, or we would have stopped being followers of a religion of revelation. Our only defense can be the fact of actually listening, and our conviction that, from time to time, we have heard the truth here. That is what we mean by being believers, for to be a man or woman of faith is simply to be under orders, as was the centurion, whose great faith consisted in the fact that he knew what it was to be under a commander (Matt. 8:9f.). This said, we may and must hear what is said to us and do our best to understand it obediently.

That God is the God of freedom is said to us in three ways, at least, in the witness of the Scriptures, and these three ways are only variations on one curious theme. We are told, first of all, that the God of Israel is just that: the God who elected and chose Israel. God exercises his freedom in freely choosing, freely electing a people, to whom—and here is the paradox—he is thereby bound, committed. By his first and essential elective act, God acts freely in such a way as to qualify, to give away, his freedom. Just as Israel is no more free to be other than God's people, so God is no longer free to be other than Israel's God. That point is etched so deeply into the Scriptures and the writings of the apostles, that everything else that is said about God there is said in the light of this one theme. Thus God is the God of a freedom that spends itself, a freedom that enters into bondage. It is the freedom of the Lord to become the servant, irrevocably and without reserve. I shall return to this more than once.

In a second way, and clearly derivative from the first, the God whose voice has been heard from time to time through the Scriptures and the writings of the apostles is one who has demonstrated his freedom by creating this world. But the subject of creation has been heard so often, and it has been so crystallized in prescientific terms, that it is difficult to hear it afresh, as we must in our day, if we are to hear it at all. Surely we cannot put the words of Genesis into competition with either side of those who weigh the evidence for and against, say, the theory of the Big Bang, or the hypothesis of an oscillating universe. In their own prescientific way, the authors and editors of Genesis, Isaiah and the Psalms wanted to say that the earth is the Lord's, that all is from him. And what if we today can only see that "all" as a process, as something unfinished? Must we then not say, as do the opening words of Genesis, that when God spoke, order was created out of chaos? But one must be honest about this: only to some extent has order been created out of chaos. And even the order, or what we are inclined to call order, is partial. The world is unfinished, not static and completed. The story is still unfolding, and its happy ending seems hardly a logical necessity. After all, even according to Genesis, God said his creation was good, not perfect. We have no way of knowing whether God could have made a perfect world from the very beginning, just as we really have no very clear idea of what a perfect creation would be like. In any case, it is not hard to find many faults with the one we do know. What else can one conclude than that God was free to begin creation, but that the results of his workings are mixed?

If the idea seems blasphemous to the traditional mind, perhaps an argument for entertaining it developed by William James in *Pragmatism* (Ralph B. Perry, ed., New York, 1965) will help make it more attractive. "Suppose," James wrote, "that the world's author put the case to you before creation, saying: 'I am going to make a world not certain to be saved, a world the perfection of which shall be conditional merely, the condition being that each several agent does its own "level best." I offer you the chance of taking part in such a world. Its safety, you see, is unwarranted. It is a real adventure, with real danger, yet it may win through. It is a social scheme of cooperative work, genuinely to be done. Will you join the procession? Will you trust yourself and trust the other agents enough to face the risk?' " James hoped that we would, for he believed it was in just such a world that we lived. Is not this the world of risk and danger and adventure of the authors of Scripture?

But a more important paradox or contradiction than this occurs in God's demonstration of his freedom to create this world, such as it is. By that very act of creation, whatever we may mean by that, God gave to his creation its own freedom and independence from him. The further unfolding of the Genesis tale makes this unavoidably clear. The Scriptures do not present us with a world that is some overflowing of the divine life, or some aspect of God himself. No, the world and the men and women in it, have been set on their own feet, for better or worse, and what is to become of them and this planet now depends to an immeasurable extent on what they decide to do, or just do without deciding.

This is to say, creation was an act that was profoundly self-limiting for the Creator. Such is the freedom of the creating God, that by freely creating, he has let the world and us be ourselves, even without him, if we so wish.

A third way in which the Scriptures and the apostolic writings tell us of this strange freedom of God is in their tale of his freeing of Israel. God is the God of freedom in that he set Israel free from slavery in Egypt. But now again, if we would see this at all clearly, we must not simply repeat familiar words but look with care at what in fact happened. Was it really *freedom* into which Israel was released? Free to worship a golden calf, free to demand a king against God's wishes, a king free to murder his trusted lieutenant in order to steal his victim's wife, Bathsheba? Is it a God of freedom who sets a people free to sell the needy for a pair of shoes, and then to be again made slaves in Babylon? Clearly the freedom of Israel is itself as much of a mystery as is God's freedom, and we shall return to that matter in the third chapter, as in the final chapter we must painfully reconsider how little Easter was a realization of that messianic kingdom of freedom which Jesus had promised his disciples.

These considerations suggest that Christians have need of reflection, the most serious and penetrating reflection, on just where they are and why, for it is all very well to speak of freedom; that is cheap enough in the "free world," because everyone assumes no one will do anything about it. That assumption will no doubt be correct if we don't even take the time to think about freedom. So let us at least think about it, however strange it may be. Clearly, the starting point must be that we are confronted with a mystery in this matter of freedom, especially when it comes to God's freedom.

In each of these three ways that the prophets and apostles tell of God's freedom, we are confronted with paradox, with ambiguity, or, as I prefer to put it, with a mystery. Before looking further at this, however, I must point out a small problem that has crept into these reflections. The language which we are using in speaking of God's freedom is the language which we use to speak of persons, ourselves. It may well be an extended or stretched use of language about persons, but it is still recognizably person-talk that provides the basis for the God-talk that we hear from the biblical writers. God is he, not it, a father—and, if you will attend closely to the figures of speech and the analogies that are used, also a mother, but not a mechanical force or a magnetic attraction.

This feature of what we hear from the Scriptures is, I believe, the proper way to put a problem which our forefathers somewhat misleadingly called the problem of anthropomorphism. That term is misleading because it forces upon us an ancient concept of *anthropos*, man, and it further works with the potentially misleading distinction between form and content. No, it is not that God is pictured in the form of a man, as the Greeks understood man, but that we find ourselves responding to what the prophets and apostles responded to as a person, and therefore using language appropriate to persons.

I think most philosophers today, and indeed most other people, take the concept "person" to be that of an individual.[2] We all have a bit of that old Platonism

[2] See P. Strawson, *Individuals*, London, 1959, for a careful presentation of the following argument.

in us, which we owe largely to St. Augustine, and we have all been in part influenced by Descartes, even if we've never read a word of him, so we are just a little bit tempted to think of persons as composites, not individuals. To that extent, we are tempted to distinguish between the self and the body, or the soul and the body, or the essential "I" and then the body which I possess, or which possesses me. But this sort of speculation is not evident in the way we habitually talk about ourselves. Normally, you cannot possibly hit my body without hitting me. Normally, if you hit my finger as I hold a nail which you are driving in, I shout, and with no misunderstanding, "Hey! You hit me!" If we attend to what we usually do with words, we will conclude that we *are* as well as *have* our bodies. Our working concept of "person" today is not a secondary and composite concept put together out of two primary concepts, body and mind, or body and soul, or body and self. Rather, we take "person" as a primary and individual concept.

Now when we hear through the biblical writings the voice of what seems to us to be a person, and when we speak of God as a person, we find ourselves committed, just by the way we are speaking and thinking, to seeing God as embodied. How could he be personal if disembodied? His body may be invisible, able to move at the speed of light, for all we know, but we speak of him as a person and therefore in some sense as embodied.

I am not forgetting, in what I have just said, the wise recommendations of so many of the early Christian Fathers,[3] that we handle our words with what I can only

[3]Chrysostom's sermons on "The Incomprehensibility of God" make the point especially strongly, but *cf.* Tertullian (*Apologeticum* 17), Clement (*Stromata* 12), and Origen (*De Principiis* I, 1).

call a certain sense of humor in this area. None of our words do justice to the One of whom we speak. To say he is wise is not at all sufficient or accurate, but, perhaps it is better to say "wise" than "stupid," the Fathers said, and I think they were right. Our words are only our own response to what we hear through the biblical authors. But if "wise" is better than "stupid," within this limitation, then surely "he" or "she" is better than "it." Personal is more appropriate than impersonal. It follows, then, that embodied, however qualified, is better than disembodied. Impassioned is better than passionless, movable is better than immovable.

I realize that these reflections lead us to think of God in ways which our forefathers considered utterly false. For them God was without body, without passions, utterly immovable. If I take issue with them, then I only dare do so because I can call as my witnesses Father Abraham and his faithful descendant, Jesus of Nazareth. If God is without passions and immovable, why pray to him at all? But Abraham not only prayed, he argued with God about the destruction of Sodom (Gen. 18:23ff.). And Jesus not only prayed to God, he is said to have sweat blood in his prayers (Luke 22:44)!

I think we must find ourselves at issue with our forefathers over this matter because we believe in persons, not in *anthropos*. What is wrong with being a person? Would we be something other? What is wrong with having a body? Would anyone prefer to be a mathematical point, a concept, an abstraction, or a memory? If we were any of those entities, would we be less limited than we are now? No, what we actually do with and in our creatureliness is another matter, but as for our creatureliness itself, our being persons, and so embodied persons, that, I think we must agree, is something we can not only accept, but, along with the authors of the first chapter of Genesis, take as a state of affairs that is good, very good. Having and being a body, being moved by pity and regret, being willing and able to change our minds, being able to remember and to forget, to threaten and to forgive, these are actions of persons, and this is the language the Bible uses about God. Since I cannot conceive of anything I would rather be than a person, I see no reason why we should regard personhood as unworthy of God.[4]

Of course if one thought of having a body as a handicap, if one would rather be some disembodied floating idea, then one may, in listening to the words of Scripture and of the apostles, be able to hear from time to time the "unvoice" of an abstraction. How such an absolute abstraction can commit itself to a particular people, rescue them from slavery, get furiously angry with them, shed tears of love over them, I do not know, and I will leave to those who wish to carry on such a theology to see what they can come up with that commends itself. I doubt they will do other than did one of the Hegelian theologians[5] of the last century who was led to conclude that, being infinite and absolute, God could not really be personal at all and is more properly, and strictly, to be denoted by "it" rather than "him." If on the other hand we hear from the biblical witnesses of a God whose freedom is such that he chooses, and thereby binds himself, that he creates and therewith sets limits on himself, that he gives freedom to his people and thereby makes his own desire and goal depen-

---

[4]In this connection, Chapter 15, "Anthropopathy," of Abraham Heschl's *The Prophets*, New York, 1962, is essential reading.
[5]Alexander Schweizer (1808–88).

dent on what men and women do, then I do not see
how we can avoid admitting that we are speaking of
God as we speak of persons, and that if God is an individual as a person is an individual then there is much
to commend the artistic, iconographic tradition that
depicts God as a kindly old Jewish patriarch. You might
improve on the picture a bit, but it points in the right
direction, for it helps you to see how St. Paul could
write that God has given us an image or picture of himself in the face of Jesus Christ (Col. 1:15; 2 Cor. 4:4, 6).

I do not want to be misunderstood, however, as
though I were saying that it is strictly accurate to say
that God is a person and so in some sense must be
thought of as embodied. The God whose freedom is
presented to us as a mystery in the words of the biblical
authors is never presented as one whom those writers
pretended to fully understand. They knew that God
was sufficiently other than men to make all our words
inaccurate to a high degree. It is always a matter of
degree, of more or less, when it comes to speaking of
God. It is of great help, however, if we can break away
from the old-fashioned and widely challenged theory of
language that views words as labels for objects, which,
when properly used, exactly match the thing labeled,
as though the purpose of language were always to de-
scribe objects. Surely God is no object to be described
for the person of faith, but one to whom a response is
due.

The question we should be asking is not whether the
words we use are accurate, but whether the words we
use are appropriate. Accuracy could only be our concern if we thought that our task were to give a description of God. (Who should want or need such a description is hard to imagine.) Then we might be forced to

develop some theory of analogy to show the logical connection between what we say of God, using human language, and God himself. But if we see that the issue of man's language about God is part of man's response to God, then we should rather be asking, Is this fitting, Is this an appropriate word to use when responding to him whom we may from time to time hear as we listen to the Scriptures and the apostolic witnesses? As a response and not a description, it seems to me appropriate that we speak of him (and maybe from time to time of her), but never of it, that we speak of God being present, occasionally, and being absent, most of the time, of his coming and going, of his desires, concerns, worries, and complaints. The biblical writers found such language appropriate, and I see no reason to decide otherwise. In that case, I accept the fact that I have been speaking as we speak of embodied persons, and so, under certain circumstances, we should be able with Job (19:21) to say, "Have pity on me, O you my friends, for the hand of God has touched me!"

Before returning to our reflections on the mystery of God's freedom, I must add to this excursus on the personhood of God that it is a radical misinterpretation of the Fathers of the Church to speak today of "God in three Persons." That is simply tri-theism, in no way a translation of what the Fathers meant with the Latin phrase *tres personae*. If we want to be loyal to their meaning and say it in modern English, we would be more accurate to say "One God, who is himself in three distinct ways."[6] If our word "person" is to be used of God, what else can we say but that God is one person?

---

[6]This was Barth's helpful translation of the original Greek word which the Latin Church attempted to express with the word *persona*.

When we say that God is free and the God of freedom, we must be careful to distinguish his personal
freedom from the idea of a theoretically absolute freedom, whatever that may mean. The idea of absolute or
unqualified freedom is at best a difficult notion to get
clear. The difficulty lies in the fact that we have learned
to use the word "freedom" always with respect to particular contexts and circumstances. The word seems by
its very use a relative term, so the attempt to abstract
it from all contexts and relationships to arrive at sheer,
absolute, unqualified freedom is a move that takes us
right out of how we speak English. The only sense such
words can have, it seems to me, is as an expression of
praise and worship. It seems appropriate as an act of
praise to find the most extreme words possible, knowing that even these are not up to saying all we might
want to say.[7] But like all other absolute and unqualified
words of praise, they get us into trouble when we try
to take them literally.

To think of God's freedom, as of his presence, as
absolute and unqualified is to make an abstraction that
is far removed from the God of whom we hear in the
biblical story. It turns the freedom of a person into the
abstract condition of an eternal state of affairs. It turns
its back on a God who is free to to do this, but not free
to do that, for the sake of a God who is so free that
everything that happens, from mongoloids and birth
defects, to random murder and rape, to Hitler's holocaust and our own Vietnam, is said to be his (or its) will.
If we conceive of God's personal freedom as abstract,
unlimited freedom, we shall be faced with the insoluble

[7]I have developed this analysis of praise at length in *The Edges of Language*,
New York, 1972, especially chapters VII and VIII.

problem of explaining why God allows the most hideous evils to exist. The biblical writers were certainly aware of evil, but apparently they realized that for some strange reason God could not, or at least did not, always act to rescue. The word that must stand in the center of our reflection here is that of the Psalmist, repeated from the cross, "My God, my God, why have you forsaken me?" (Ps. 22:1).

There is, I think we must say, a strange mystery about God's freedom. It is a mystery, I repeat, and not a puzzle. Puzzles are intellectual problems; mysteries have to do with our whole existence. Puzzles get solved; mysteries must be lived with. Nor is a mystery an unknown to be found out by thought or experiment. Puzzles get resolved and unknowns get discovered. But when one has found out all that can be found out about a mystery, the mystery is still there. It does not go away. Indeed, not all that much discovering is needed, for this mystery stands revealed. What the biblical witnesses make all too plain to us is the strangeness, the foreignness of God's freedom. The more clearly we see it, the more it scares us as a mystery, for it seems to contradict our usual ideas of freedom. Presented with the freedom of the God of Abraham, Isaac and Jacob, we may well want to say, "But that's not freedom! That's not what we mean by freedom!" And as we are Americans, that is true; but as we are Christians, it is reason for reflection.

There would not be this mystery if we made God over again in our own image and after our likeness, and indeed when men do this, and they do, there is no mystery about the God they end up with. A God who is conceived of as what we think God ought to be has an unmysterious freedom. The God of Feuerbach, or what Feuerbach took the Christian idea of God to be, a God who is a projection of our own best ideals, or the God which Freud thought we projected out of our infantile needs may be unmysteriously independent, absolutely, unqualifiedly free. But the God of Abraham, Isaac and Jacob, the God of Moses and of Jesus Christ has another sort of freedom. His freedom is more like that of one who goes to jail to serve the sentence of another. God's freedom is that of one who puts himself at the mercy of others. It is the mark of the freedom of Israel's God that he lets it be qualified again and again, as the story of Abraham illustrates.

The story of Abraham is that of one chosen for a task on which the whole future of God's purposes depended. Without Abraham's faith, where would those plans have been? And having given Abraham the child of promise, again a free gift on which the whole future of that promise depended, God put it all to risk in sending Abraham on that strange trip to Mount Moriah (Gen. 22). It is no doubt true to say that Abraham is the one who risked everything, but it is surely just as true to say that God himself risked his whole enterprise in those events.[8]

We should also consider that early Christian hymn which St. Paul made use of in his letter to the community of believers in Philippi (Phil. 2:6–11). We hear there of a strange freedom to surrender freedom. Jesus, in his overriding concern for our interests, represented

[8]There is a rabbinic tradition that God's power depends on Israel's obedience. A saying of Rabbi Judah ben Simon is an example: "When the Israelites do God's will, they add to the power of God on high. When the Israelites do not do God's will, they, as it were, weaken the great power of God on high." Cited in Montefiore & Loewe, *A Rabbinic Anthology*, New York, 1974 (1938), p. 34. *Cf.* pp. 34–35 for other examples.

God's way in a manner utterly unlike what we might expect of a majestically free sovereign: he emptied himself, poured himself out, taking up the position of a slave like other slaves, becoming as dependent as any man, and doing God's will even to the point of dying a criminal's death. Easter is presented as God's certification that this strange freedom to become a slave is the divine form of freedom.[9]

It was evidently the view of the early apostolic community that what had happened in the life, death and resurrection of Jesus was not some little addition to what they knew about God. Of course they thought that what happened in these events was not utterly contrary to what had always been true about God, that this strange mystery of a freedom that was self-denying, that put itself in jeopardy, that risked its own exercise in order that God's creatures might be free, was what had already been pointed to in the story of Abraham, in the escape from Egypt, in the gift of Torah at Sinai, and in the words of the prophets. But now, once for all time, in the clearest possible way, God, they were convinced, had laid his heart bare.

God is faithful, but he is faithful to himself. So God is free to do a new thing, a radically new thing, in order that something new should happen to his creation. He had always shown his freedom to change his mind, not to be bound to what he had planned. The glorious but frightening dialogue of Abraham with God over the fate of Sodom, and the story of God's change of mind in the face of Nineveh's repentance, so exasperating to the prophet Jonah, are cases in point. But above all, it

[9]I have made use of the essay on *morphe* (form) in *Theologisches Wörterbuch zum Neuen Testament,* IV, pp. 758ff.

was this new self-disclosure in the event of Jesus Christ which the apostles took as the definitive sign that God's freedom is freedom to do the radically new, the utterly unexpected.

If that is what we hear, then I suggest that our appropriate response must be to set aside whatever ideas we have about God's freedom and look squarely at the face of that slave-leader of slaves who refused to be called good, who ended his life with all the freedom of a man hanging from a cross. He called his disciples to come with him, and when they would not or could not go further in this path of mutual dependence, he went the last steps for them.

How can we begin to pull this strange picture together? I think it would not be far wrong to say that the whole story, from the call of Abraham to the appearances of the risen Jesus, and reflected back into a story of creation and a covenant with Noah and ahead into an unimaginable victory, is a story that opens up the mystery of God's freedom. The word we hear is that this God, regardless of whatever ideas men may have about him, this God refuses to be without his creatures, without men and women. He refuses, that is, to be God without us sharing in all that he has to give us. The mystery of his freedom, then, is that God will not exercise his freedom, he refuses to be free, apart from us.

Does it make sense to say this, to say that God has freely renounced his freedom, that it is his will, freely, not to exercise his freedom, indeed no longer to be free until we are? Does it make sense to say that God, too, longs for freedom, that he is waiting for us to exercise the freedom for which we were set free? Above all, we ought to make clear what would be our grounds for speaking in this way, for saying that God created us for freedom, and that now he waits, in as much pain and agony as any of his enslaved and oppressed creatures, for a freedom that he has called us to realize, his freedom now dependent upon ours.

Grounds for speaking in this way are to be found by listening to the strange words which the apostle Paul wrote in an open letter to the community of believers in Rome. He had never seen these people, but it was reasonable of him to suppose that in Rome as in Greece, Asia Minor and Palestine, the community was made up perhaps in good part of proletarians, the oppressed of the Roman system.[10] That the earliest Christian communities had not many wise, not many well-born, that they really included the proletariat and the scum of Roman society is one of those little items we often ignore, but it is there to see for all who can read, and it is becoming one of the largest and most difficult facts of the ecumenical situation in the world today. For the oppressed Christians of Latin America have heard this fact anew and are repeating it loudly.[11] And so are the oppressed Christians in other places. And the question is how they are going to be able to tolerate the bourgeois Christianity of North America and Europe without tearing the Church in two.

As proletarians, the communities to which Paul wrote had few if any illusions about the system of their society and their own place in it. They knew perfectly

[10]Karl Kautsky's recently republished *Foundations of Christianity*, New York, 1972, argues that the early communities were almost entirely proletarian. For a more balanced assessment see the essay by Heinz Kressig in *Eirene: Studia Graeca et Latina*, VI, Prague, 1967, pp. 91–100. I am indebted to Dr. Scott Bartchy for this last reference.

[11]For an example of what they hear, see Gustavo Gutierrez, *A Theology of Liberation*, Maryknoll, N.Y., 1973.

well that the system was not free, and that it offered them oppression, not freedom. It would never have crossed their minds to think of the Roman system as "the Free World," in contrast to the barbarians to the north or those coming out of Asia who were to push against the empire. The Roman world was not free. It was, in its higher levels, exceedingly wealthy. It commanded a high level of technology, combined with a wide-flung and powerful defense network armed with the latest weapons. But little of that seems to have been represented in these early communities. Accommodation with the system was to come at a later time, but you can catch something of the character of these communities in their early days by recalling that they preserved as sacred some words which they claimed, rightly or wrongly, to be those of Jesus himself: "Blessed are you poor, for yours is the kingdom of God. Blessed are you that are hungry now, for you shall be satisfied. . . . But woe to you that are rich, for you have received your consolation. Woe to you that are full now, for you shall hunger." (Luke 6:20f.,24f.) And the people that Paul wrote to were also to preserve other words, which they would claim to be those of Jesus's mother: "He [God] has scattered the proud in the imagination of their hearts, He has put down the mighty from their thrones and exalted those of low degree; He has filled the hungry with good things, and the rich He has sent empty away." (Luke 1:51–53) And further, the community to which Paul wrote was also one of those that would preserve yet other words as sacred, which were claimed, rightly or wrongly, to have been those of James, the brother of Jesus: "Come now, you rich, weep and howl for the miseries that are coming upon you. Your riches have rotted and your garments are moth-eaten. Your gold and silver have rusted, and their rust will be evidence against you and will eat your flesh like fire. You have laid up treasure for the last days? Behold, the wages of the workers who worked your fields and which you kept back by fraud cry out, and the cry of the workers has reached the ears of the Lord of Hosts. You have lived on the earth in luxury and in pleasure; you have fattened your hearts in a day of slaughter." (*James* 5:1–5)

These having been preserved as sacred writings by these communities, there is something to be said for calling them proletarian communities. Moreover, these texts may play a role in defining a developing ecumenical problem for the times ahead. For one can well imagine that there are Christians in Latin America, in Africa, in Vietnam, not to speak of black Christians in America, for whom these are still sacred writings. And they have begun to wonder whether the white Christians of North America can also sing that Magnificat with Mary, or hold those other words sacred. Their question may help us to hear more sensitively what St. Paul wrote.

To the oppressed of Rome, Paul wrote that they were not alone in their suffering. Now, he said, the whole environment, the whole ecosystem groans like a woman in labor along with you, agonizing for the birth of your freedom, the glorious liberty of the sons of God. But far more than that, the Creator Spirit, God himself, groans with us in this same longing for that great day of liberation! (Romans 8:19–24, 28). Since St. Paul wrote to such people and said such things, how else are we to respond to what is to be heard here than to say that God's freedom waits upon our own?

I think, however, that we must press this point fur-

ther by asking what were St. Paul's grounds for writing
what he did. The answer to this, evidently, is the very
preaching of Jesus, taken in conjunction with the
events that followed. Jesus came preaching that the
great and glorious messianic age, the reign of God, was
about to begin, when the mighty would be overthrown,
the poor would be raised up and would share the
wealth, and the sufferings of the present evil system
would be done away with. He was understandably at-
tacked by the power structure for such revolutionary
notions. And then, so strangely, so evidently beyond
the understanding of his followers, he appeared victori-
ous. The victory, however, was utterly ambiguous, for
the messianic age did not arrive. What happened on
Easter (and I shall discuss this more fully in the fourth
chapter) could more accurately be called a token of the
new era that Jesus had proclaimed and promised, a
small down payment, to use a term of St. Paul's (2 Cor.
1:22; 5:5). Easter provided just a hint of what God
wanted, but evidently it was not to be accomplished
without us. In the meantime—and it has been a "meantime" that has now lasted nineteen and a half centuries
—St. Paul urged that it is our time, time for us to start
doing the walking (Rom. 6:4). For freedom Christ has
set us free, he wrote. Theologians have made a remarkably static paradox out of that, but we can read it
dynamically. I think we can hear in these words that for
freedom, for the sake of the coming great goal of God's
promise, we have been set free to join God in longing
for this, and set free to start working for it. Until that
movement on our part seriously begins, then these long
centuries of God's delay continue to stretch out before
us into an inglorious future of oppression and decay.
This, as I think we can hear it, is the mystery of God's

freedom, that he has made the final freedom of himself and his whole creation dependent upon us.

Our subject is the *mystery* of freedom, and more specifically in this first chapter, the mystery of God's freedom. I do not want anything I have said to diminish the force of that word "mystery." What we say in speaking of God's freedom is not and can never be other than or more than our response to that which is strange, foreign to us. Moreover, if our words are our only response, our total response, then they are an inappropriate response from those who are under orders to be doers of the word, not just hearers. That is the mystery of theology, if you will, that its goal is to wither away, to be unnecessary. Jeremiah's vision of the goal (Jer. 31:33–34) was of a time in which we would not have to ask critically about the appropriateness of our words about God, since in that day we would be living lives appropriate to the goal. In the interim, however, we have need to reflect critically on what we say as one aspect of our appropriate response to God's strange freedom, which has ceased to be active until we exercise our freedom.

As a response, our words, even at their best, may hardly be any better than those which I would like to imagine being spoken by my dog, could she speak, as she told her canine friends of her master's freedom. As words of affection and praise, she might well say, "He can do anything!" In point of fact, she has seen me weep tears of frustration. I do not believe we can know the Holy One of Israel much better. There have been those, however, who thought they saw the glory of God in the weeping face of Christ. If they are right, then to that extent, it does make sense to speak of divine frustration and of the mystery of a freedom abandoned until that time when God's children rise up to do battle with him against all that denies the freedom of the sons of God. For Christians in America, that opens up a large and serious agenda. In a world that groans for freedom, we have been set free to know our situation and to accept our calling to work for that for which the whole creation is in labor pains. The mystery of this is that God has chosen not to act for us but has commanded us to be his fellow workers. It is the mystery of God's freedom that he will not exercise it apart from us. The freedom of God waits upon us. Clearly, the name of that sort of freedom is love.

2. THE MYSTERY OF HUMAN FREEDOM

In the first chapter, our reflections on the subject of freedom led to the conclusion that God's freedom is mysterious in this way: that God is not and will not be free apart from us. We turn now to the other side of the picture, the mystery of human freedom. At an early stage of our modern era, Jean Jacques Rousseau began his famous essay, *The Social Contract,* with the observation that man is born free, but everywhere he is in chains. With those words, if not his further development of them, Rousseau, like Karl Marx, revealed his roots in the biblical story of Israel's history. The thesis has two sides: man is made for freedom, but this freedom he does not have.

In important respects, both the "free world," the world of special-interest socialism, and also the communist world, the world of state socialism, agree at least that man is born for a freedom which he does not have. The Christian as well can agree with the capitalists and the communists on this matter. But of course the special-interest-socialist and the state-socialist worlds differ radically in their understanding of what is the cause of human slavery or oppression, because they differ radically on the nature of that freedom for which they both say man was born. And if a Marxian analysis has any merit, then we could apply it to both sides and find that their views of freedom reflect exactly their respective social conditions. In special-interest socialism, the essential concern for freedom will be that of the special interests, whereas in state socialism, the freedom which seems finally to matter is that of the state and its bureaucratic apparatus. The subject of our concern as reflective Christians, however, is neither special interests nor the state, but persons, human beings. I shall argue that from the perspective of Israel's history, a third understanding of human freedom must follow, and so a third understanding of the problem, of the cause of our lack of freedom. I shall therefore not talk further about the other two views, except by contrast as one or the other may tempt us to confuse the message of Christianity with that of either of these alternative diagnoses of and prescriptions for the human predicament. We shall focus, then, on the particular way in which the biblical writings lead us to hear that man is born for freedom, yet is everywhere in chains.

Although the Genesis stories are logically and historically secondary to the primary biblical story of human freedom, the story of the Exodus, it will be convenient to look at them just because they are so definitely shaped by the faith of the Exodus and Sinai.[1] In the Genesis stories of mankind's origin, man is created as a couple. As the couple of male and female, this creature is said to be in the image of God. "In the image of God

[1]This judgment is derived from G. von Rad, *Das erste Buch Mose* (ATD,2), Göttingen, 1953.

He created him; male and female He created them,"
runs the Hebrew couplet (Gen. 1:27). And this new
creature, the human couple, is given dominion over the
animals, and it is all judged to be very good.

The second creation story (Gen. 2:4–25) presents
man's origins in a slightly different way. First the male
is made alone and given a fine garden to take care of.
But at once it becomes evident that this is inadequate,
a half-way creation, for the man alone is not fully himself. After repeated attempts to see if the company of
any of the various animals will satisfy him, the Lord
finally makes Adam's "significant other," as we say today, out of his own self. Then all is well. They are two;
yet, being of the same bone and flesh, they are one.

And now the new creature, the couple, naked before
their maker and exposed to each other, live in harmony
with their environment, for they have the assignment
to be caretakers of the environment. They are there as
shepherds of creation, not without time to stroll in the
cool of the evening with their God. So in two comple-
mentary pictures we are presented with our first biblical images of human freedom. I need hardly point out
how radically these images differ from the ideals and
above all the actual aims of the social systems of East
and West. Man is neither primarily a worker, or inven-
tor, or constructor, as Marxists see him, nor an individual producer and above all consumer, as our western
system defines him. He is primarily couple, and then,
along with that, this couple is a caretaker. Yet both
stories are marked by a not-yet; they imply or hint at
a future. Something is going to happen: freedom is
what will be, not what is already.

I call as the second witness, father Abraham, the
father of all believers, as St. Paul saw him, Kier-

kegaard's knight of faith. Of what sort was his freedom, this man of God's good pleasure? Well, he was (and I believe that must be a part of what we are to hear about human freedom from the biblical writers), he was one who walked by faith, setting out with Sarah his wife on the strangest journey known to history, having no map of any sort and without even a hint as to his destination (Gen. 12:1). He went forth as one not knowing where he was to go, the author of Hebrews has it (11:8), as one compelled and driven by that of which he could not speak. Is this what it is to be free? No real estate equity, no insurance, no social security or pension plan, setting out into the unknown in your old age: is that what anyone wants?

Then in their extreme old age, Abraham and Sarah had a child, the child that was promised, the child on whom the whole future of God and man depended. I think we must see that God's future depended on this child too, or else we will not be able to hear the story as it unfolds. God's future too depended on this child because in his promise to Abraham that Abraham's descendants would be a blessing to all humanity, God had committed himself. Had this child been destroyed, God's own desire would have been destroyed, his own promise annulled, his own plans frustrated. In a way that threatened himself as well as Abraham, therefore, God placed his own and Abraham's future in Abraham's hands: he tested Abraham by asking him to sacrifice his only son. So once again, Abraham went on a journey without destination, taking with him his son and a servant. In stubborn obedience he set out to sacrifice the boy, only to be stopped at the last moment. And then, it was at that point, in the very act of stubbornly or woodenly doing what he would have longed not to do, that Abraham was pronounced the free man of God's choosing. Is that what we mean by freedom? If this way were offered to us, would we dare to walk it? Is this freedom, this white-hot burning coal, something that we would dare or care to pick up with our bare hands?

I pass over that greatest of all images of freedom in the Bible, the Exodus, because, like its parallel in the New Testament, the event of Easter, its ambiguities are so complex, its mystery so worthy of our attention, that I wish to reserve consideration of it for the following chapters. Instead, let us consider that figure whose history the apostolic community saw as the embodiment of the plan and purpose of the God of freedom, of the One who gave his name to Moses as "I am becoming what I am becoming," or "I shall be what I shall be," the God who waits for man, namely, the man Jesus of Nazareth.[2] Of this man, said the unknown author of the fourth Gospel, if he makes you free, you shall be free indeed, which parallels St. Paul's cry to the community in Galatia: for freedom Christ has set us free! Behind these two lines lies the presumption for Christian faith that this man defines and holds up for reflection the ultimate goal of human freedom.

But what is presented to us? It is a figure as unlikely as one could imagine, a stranger to our world, misunderstood by his closest associates and hunted down by church and state. He was the leader of a band of vagabonds, without papers or credentials, lacking place or

[2]The following passages are behind this formulation: Eph. 1:9–10; John 1:14; Col. 1:19–20; and Phil. 2:6. *Cf.* the Christology of Call and Response developed in my *The Secular Meaning of the Gospel*, New York, 1963, pp. 47–55 (omitting the last sentence).

possesions, hunted by the police and denounced by ecclesiastical authority. He was a man whose haunts were "skid row" and whose language was revolutionary, and he was killed by the military in the name of national security.

What strange sort of freedom is this, this free will that chooses not to be free but to be the slave of God's plan? Jesus lost his life in service to a cause which the apostolic writers call the new era, a new age, or the coming reign of God. Looking to the immediate commencement of this new age, he had no respect for the powers or the establishment of the old age. Rulers and ecclesiastics meant nothing to him, for they were passing away. He had no respect for the prerogatives and pomp of power.

Nor did he respect the claims of his natural family and relatives. Only his new family mattered, those who like him set their eye upon the coming age and did not look back (Luke 9:62). And he had no respect at all for that great god of our culture, private property. Your coat was for clothing him who had none, your food was for those with nothing (Matt. 5:40, 42; 25:35f.). In fact in the parable of the unjust steward—unjust, that is, only by the standards of the present age—he commended the steward for giving away someone else's property, his master's, for the sake of the radically different values of the age that was coming (Luke 16:1–9).

Above all, the figure presented to us is that of one who would not go his way alone. His life was a perpetual calling out, drawing to himself, reaching out, toward the poor and the wealthy, even if few wealthy responded; to the healthy and the sick, even if few healthy would listen (Mark 2:17); to the religious and the irreligious, although the religious were mostly too anxious to be free to move; even to the living and the dead, and the dead seemed to have heard him even more clearly than the living (John 11:43f.). To all these he reached out, calling them to come with him in his way into the new era. Follow me, was his call; the new age is at hand. Those who came found themselves bound to him and to each other in a new communism of love, suddenly free to leave family, friends, possessions and status, free to let the dead go bury their dead. And woe to those bound to family, possessions, national pride, social status, and the past, for they would never be free. Such is the free man presented in Jesus of Nazareth. This is the freedom that he set before his followers as a new way into a new era. Freedom is indeed a Christian goal, *this* freedom, but do we any of us really want *this* sort of freedom?

"Apart from me you can do nothing," one apostolic writer has Jesus say to his disciples (John 15:5). They were evidently conscious that their freedom depended on his. But more striking is the reverse side of the coin: without them he could do nothing! Without the response of faith, he could do no mighty works, it is reported (Mark 6:5–6). Unless his disciples came along with him in his way, he seems to have been unwilling or unable to proceed. In binding his disciples to himself, he bound himself to them, even to the point of final separation, where he vowed that he would not drink again until he could drink with them once more in the new age (Mark 14:25). Until the freedom of the new era would dawn for them, his freedom would not be realized.

All too obviously for his disciples, the new era did not come, the new age to which Jesus had looked did not arrive, not right away, and not after years of waiting, either! This terrible delay was an oppressive worry for the early community of believers, and it is there for any to read in their writings, no matter how thoroughly the succeeding generations of Christians have shut their eyes to it and failed to think through its implications. The failure of Christians to remember what Jesus had promised about the new era, the new and imminent messianic age, and their refusal to go on being bothered by its delay runs, in augmented form, parallel to Israel's milder failure to recall that the land into which they came from Egypt was but a token of what God had promised. Was it, then, perhaps guilt over their own failure to mark the difference between where they were and what had been promised them that led Christians so early into a virulent anti-Jewish harping on Judaism's lesser failure? If so, how accurately Jesus had predicted that the brother with a beam stuck in his own eye would expend such efforts to call attention to the speck in Judaism's eye. But that is a matter to return to in the following chapters. On the basis of these biblical images of freedom, we are now in a position to define the characteristics of human freedom so that these may properly be a Christian goal.

When we listen to these biblical portrayals of human freedom, what stands out as strange, foreign, difficult to accept because so different from what we hear all around us, is the mutuality of human freedom. The mystery of human freedom seems to match or reflect the mystery of divine freedom. Just as God will not be free apart from us, so we are told that we shall not be free without our fellow creatures, and they will not be free without us. We are bound together in the structure of God's creation in such a way that there simply cannot be such a thing as individual freedom. We shall all go

free together, or we are all locked into bondage together. Whatever we have entered into in being alive
as human beings in this world, it is all of a piece: God,
mankind and the whole of creation groan together in
bondage, and we shall all march into freedom together
or not at all. That, in its largest form, is the mystery of
human freedom. The whole creation, and also creation's Creator Spirit, groan together, and the whole
creation will be liberated together. Anything less than
this is slavery masquerading as freedom—and the
masks are all around us.

Christians in America have special need of a guide,
a help by the aid of which we can learn to pull off the
false faces of freedom that play around us and seek to
seduce us away from true freedom. Such a guide is to
be found in a critical principle which may be formu-
lated thus: any theology which reinforces the powers-
that-be of this present old age is to that extent a false,
deceptive theology. And why is this principle to be
respected? Because such a theology that did business
with this old era would be in conflict with him who
called us out of the old age into the new age of light and
freedom. The old age and all that supports it is the age
of death, and we are called, also in our reflection, in our
theologizing, to the new age. Therefore, a theology of
a freedom that can be a Christian goal cannot, without
contradiction, reinforce the perverted concepts of freedom that operate in the old age. For us Americans who
are Christians and happen to live in and be surrounded
by the American way of life, it is especially important
that we distinguish between the freedom of the American way of life and the freedom of him who is the way,
the truth and the life. We live in a culture that makes
much of freedom, that tells us we live in the land of the

free. As has been said, we live in a land in which both
bums and millionaires are free to sleep under bridges
and scrounge for crusts of bread in trash cans.

If there is going to be a genuinely American theology, as a theology of freedom, it will have to make its
way, quite consciously, in conflict with another idea of
freedom. For there is, assuredly, a vision of human freedom which may and ought to be a Christian goal, just
as there is a vision of human freedom which cannot and
may not be a Christian goal. Before we agree too read-
ily that freedom is a Christian goal, let us be clear about
what we mean by freedom, and so, let us be clear about
the masks of freedom that cover the face of enslavement. For as Ernst Bloch has warned us, "Under Neo-
Capitalism, the old servitudes are only padded and
painted over, while under State Communism, they are
only congealed and renamed."[3]

Over against the images of freedom which we have
seen in the biblical story, there stands before us another
image of freedom. This mask of freedom may be distin-
guished by one decisive feature, which has two inter-
related aspects. The first aspect is the thesis that I can
have freedom alone, by myself; the second is that freedom means that I may do what I want. Or to put it in
another form, freedom can be mine, though all the
world go to hell, and this freedom is my own self-reali-
zation within myself, according to my own inner needs.
(I do not know whether the many faddish imitations of
eastern disciplines of meditation and introspection can
in fact achieve even this sort of freedom. I only know
that if any of them succeed, then they lead to something that stands in radical contradiction to what we

[3] *Man On His Own,* New York, 1970, p. 91.

have to hear from the biblical hints of human freedom; and I would add that they are also far removed from what I understand to be the true liberation of Buddhism's bodhisattvas.) In order to be clear about the meaning of human freedom, therefore, we need to distinguish the corporate freedom for which Christians are called to hope from the individualized freedom defined by the United States Constitution.

The Constitution, according to its Preamble, was established in order to "secure the Blessings of Liberty." This kind of freedom can be preserved because it is already a possession. But if as Christians we are to hope for freedom as a goal, then we are called to long for something we do not now possess. Knowledge that we have already acquired cannot, by the simplest rules of language, be a goal for us. Money in the pocket, experiences already had, abilities already acquired cannot be goals. A goal is by definition something not in hand, something one does not have. So either we have freedom already, and so it cannot be a goal for Christians or anyone else, or, on the contrary, it is or can be a goal, and that means that we do not have it already. And if this is true, then we need to clear up the fuzz in our thinking that leads us to think that what we have is freedom. Swimming in a social ethos that whispers or shouts to us continually that we already have these freedoms, that we are already free, that we are in the free world, Christians have to stop and sort things out a bit, to get quite clear about the difference between that which this old era calls freedom, and that other, new, different freedom of the new age, the one we don't have, and so the freedom that both can and must be our goal as Christians. What we are offered by our society is freedom to fool around in our spare time, freedom to go to the church of our choice on our day off, freedom to read whatever the society is willing to place in our hands, freedom to chat with our friends, and even to join a nice harmless demonstration every so often. But this free-time, vacation-time freedom, this is surely not that freedom for which Christ has set us free.

What is so dangerously misleading about the Bill of Rights and the whole Constitution is that they never speak directly about the real powers with which we must wrestle and which have us in their control. We are presented with a picture that contains the government in its various little branches, and then a rather typically eighteenth-century romantic vision of the individual, and of the people as a group of sovereign individuals. The citizen or citizens, and the government: that is all we hear of directly. Only mentioned indirectly, as that which the Congress may regulate, is commerce. (At the other extreme, mention is also made indirectly of the utterly powerless, those "other persons," other, that is, than "free persons," who count as 60 percent of a person for the purposes of determining the number of representatives from each state and the distribution of the tax burden. Women too counted for this purpose, but they had no more power than those 60-percent-persons, the slaves.) But when we now look around us and consider where the power really lies, the forces that control and govern not just our private lives, not simply our employment and income, but the whole economy of the land, and therefore the major policies, domestic and foreign, of this the most powerful nation on the earth, we must wonder how seriously we should take that document which so carefully spells out the rules for our free-time activities of politics and private pursuits. When it comes to those forces, not least of which are the gigantic transnational corporations which have for so long shaped the world into rich industrial centers and whole continents of poverty and misery, of them we hear next to nothing in our Constitution. Whether we have any freedom in the face of these real powers, the Bill of Rights does not say. No, the Constitution speaks only of citizens and the government.

Our warfare, the author of Ephesians warned us, is not with such puny flesh and blood as we saw paraded before us in shame during the Watergate show. Our warfare is rather with principalities and powers, with spiritual hosts of wickedness in higher places than the White House (Eph. 6:12). The issue of freedom which that passage poses is on a cosmic scale. Now many or perhaps most of us may find it difficult if not impossible to grasp and think through our human situation on so vast a scale as the cosmic. But even if that seems beyond us, we can at least think through our situation on some fuller scale than that of the citizen and his government, which the Constitution offers. When today we speak of "the establishment," or better, of "the system," we are struggling, I believe, to find some way to indicate those more basic, more pervasive and more powerful forces that determine our human condition. Political institutions may indeed reflect the disposition of these more pervasive forces which we call the system, but it is the system which runs politics, not the reverse. Not many of us have much confidence that a political election is really going to change anything. The reluctant retirement of one president and the forced resignation of his successor still leave us just about where we were, when you get down to the basics of both domestic and foreign policy.

In the light of these facts, it is dawning on more and

more Christians that the issue of human freedom not only cannot be worked out on the individual level, it cannot even be resolved as a political issue. The issue of freedom is one which touches the whole system. And I think we are justified in coming to this conclusion. All of our social and political as well as our individual experience supports this view, but more fundamentally, this view of the matter corresponds with the voice which echoes in the biblical words about human freedom: freedom is not an individual matter. Let unenlightened Americans talk about our individual freedom, and our personal freedoms. As Christians, we have no right to talk that way. It is contrary to the voice that some of us have heard, as well as to our social experience. The freedom which is a Christian goal, the freedom for which Christians long and pray is universal, not individual, systemic, not personal. For we have heard it made clear again and again that the freedom for which Christ has set us free is freedom together. There cannot be this sort of freedom in Washington, D.C., as long as it does not exist in Santiago de Chile, Madrid and Seoul. And likewise, it cannot exist in Moscow when it does not exist in Warsaw, Prague and Berlin. Either we shall be free together or we shall not be free at all. This, as we saw, was the first clear aspect of the freedom to which we are pointed by the biblical story.

One implication of this truth for our own immediate context is that there can be no liberation for blacks if there is not also and at the same time, a liberation for whites. Some of us whites have slowly learned to listen to what blacks have been saying: this country doesn't have a black problem, or, as it used to be called, a Negro problem, just as the Germans of the thirties did not have a Jewish problem. They thought they had a Jewish problem, but after six million Jews had been killed, the problem, oddly enough, still seemed to be there. No, the problem they had was a Nazi German problem. So in our case, the problem is not a black one. It is white. And white America has to get over its white problem, which is no simple matter, it having been bred into whites through the centuries-long experience and habits of domination and oppression. When you have been standing on the backs of other men for century after century, you do not easily learn what it is like to walk on the ground as other men do. You aren't free to just start doing that. And until whites are liberated from what has happened to their minds and souls through centuries of being oppressors, black liberation is going to be an illusion.

To take another area, there is not going to be much in the way of women's liberation without there being at the same time a men's liberation. The problem is not simply that of women having slipped into a role of passivity, subservience and dependence from which they have to free themselves. The problem is that they have to live in the same world with men who have become enslaved to roles of domination, so smoothly disguised under the various faces of solicitude, protectiveness and support. If men are not liberated from such attitudes and habits, where will women's liberation lead, except to a rival enslavement to those identical false images which hold men captive in our society? What we have to hope and work for is human liberation, women and men together, and until we see the dimensions of this full problem, we shall go on misunderstanding the nature of the separate problems. The freedom for which as Christians we can hope and work as a goal, however, is and can only be one that we shall find together, or not at all.

To pick one last issue with a thousand ramifications,

the poor will not be liberated from the oppressive bonds of poverty until at the same time the rich are liberated from the oppressive bonds of wealth, and this is as true of nations and societies as it is of individual classes within any one society.[4] This is a way of putting the matter that sounds strange and would not ordinarily come to mind were we not trying to reflect on the situation from the vantage point pressed upon us by the voice we occasionally hear from the biblical writings. Apart from that voice, we might want to say that if the poor are to be liberated from their poverty, then we, the relatively rich, shall have to be persuaded to give up our wealth voluntarily, or else be forced to give it up. But when we look at the matter in the light of the solidarity of freedom, we have to say it differently: at issue is our being liberated of our wealth as individuals and as a class, and of this country being liberated of its wealth and power and ability to dominate the international scene. We can begin to see that what binds us to a system which perpetuates the poverty of the Third World, which has seen to it that the disparity between the wealthy, industrial nations and the poor and oppressed nations persists and grows, is that from which we have to be liberated. We can begin to see that we have become slaves to a system and so to a pattern of thought, according to the logic of which we can only think of India, and Indochina, and Brazil, and Upper Volta as having to become as we are. That is the logic from which we have to be set free. The freedom which is and can and must be a goal for Christians is a freedom for all, a freedom of which we Americans are in as much

[4]Gustavo Gutierrez made this point in his *A Theology of Liberation*. See especially pp. 276 and 285, n.56.

need as those who starve to death and die from torture in the lands we control by our wealth.

"Love God," said Saint Augustine, "and do as you please." Indeed, love God, and only then and in that context, do as you please, for then your pleasure will be to do what pleases God. Being free is not doing what we want to do. Being free, in the sense in which as Christians we are permitted and commanded to long for it, is being in that condition in which we do what is right, what is God's will, and only then our will, as we have gladly become slaves of God, whose service is perfect freedom. Paradoxical as it may sound, we shall be more free when we are being forced to do what we do not want, like Abraham pushed out of Ur of the Chaldees or pushed to sacrifice his son on Mount Moriah, or like Moses forced to go back to Egypt to lead out his people, or like Jesus compelled to drink that cup which he so clearly did not want in the Garden of Gethsemene. That is freedom, not what we hear from every side in this society, from this old age that is passing away. When our wealth, our power, our prestige as Americans, as whites, as a superpower, as the guardian and leader of "the free world," when this is torn away from us by powers we are inclined to regard as our enemies, then, as Christians, will we be able to lift up our heads, and even shout for joy, because we are being led into freedom, against our natural wills? Abraham, Moses, Christ himself put that question to us and beg us to say yes, to accept, to long for even more, to work for the freedom for which Christ has set us free.

Strange claim, that: for freedom, Christ has set us free. For freedom, for the sake of freedom, in order that there might be freedom, so that we might long and agonize for freedom, we have been set free. Set free?

How can we long for it if we have been set free already?
Clearly, we could and would not. Then it must mean
just this, that we have been freed only in this special
sense: we have barely tasted the freedom that God wills
for us, but at least we are free to long for it, to desire
it above all else. For clearly, the biblical voice speaks to
us of freedom which we do not have, of that which can
only be, but must also be for us, a goal.

We are not yet free. That the biblical writers know
full well. How so? Why are we not free? Because we live
in the age that is not the age of freedom, the old age,
the age that includes all of recorded history to our day,
and on until a new age shall begin, the age of the Messiah, of the Kingdom or reign of God. This old age, that
new age; this world, and after it, the next. We must not
be misled by centuries of misinterpretation to think of
this in Neo-Platonic terms as one age below and then,
concurrently with it, running along parallel in time to
this life, another life, another, invisible world one thousand miles above it up above the clouds. No, like the
twenty-first century, or the age of solar energy heating,
the age to come is the age or period of history which is
not yet. It is the world invisible because it is not here
yet, invisible in just the way the twenty-first century is
invisible. The reign of God, like the reign of Queen
Elizabeth the Third is not yet, is coming; only, unlike
the reign of Elizabeth III, it is a reign that is announced
with promise, the age of human freedom, all of us together. Until that age comes, and we will have to reflect
on this at length in the remaining chapters, we live in
the old age of bondage, the age in which we are not
free. That future is the age of freedom, of the freedom
for which we long. And yet, St. Paul said, for this very
freedom, that we may long for that freedom, Christ has
set us free.

We come then to the final, and to my mind, the most exciting, the most staggering mystery of human freedom. It is a mystery of human freedom that it is corporate, systemic, universal, so that none can be free without all the others. It is a further mystery of our freedom that it does not consist in each person doing whatever he or she wants, but that together we do what others want and thereby all of us do what God wants. But beyond all of that comes the final mystery of human freedom: some of us, a few of humanity, God's Israel, have been already set free in a strictly limited but genuine sense, to see, to hear, to understand, to reflect and so to act, because we now know at least a bit of what freedom is all about. This strange freedom may be considered in three ways, and in each we shall find that it bears the marks of the mystery of human freedom which we have been considering. We shall conclude this chapter, then by considering briefly the mystery of the freedom of God's people, and the freedom of faith, and the freedom of theology, in their common qualifications of being corporate in character, and of being activity not according to our own will.

It is the mystery of human freedom that we are not free, and yet for the sake of that freedom which we do not yet have, we have already been set free. Luther in his little book on the freedom of the Christian had it just right when he said that we are free to be the slave of every other person. Our freedom as Christians consists in our knowing that we are all made for freedom, that we do not yet have this freedom, and that we are nonetheless permitted to start acting now as if we were free. Because our context is one of bondage we do not succeed at all well in acting as free persons, yet we are invited to pick ourselves up and keep starting again. We are free to try to do as we would if we really loved

God with all our heart and mind and strength. We are free deliberately to seek not our own good, but the good of others. And if we do not exercise our highly limited, extremely qualified liberty in this way, then even the little that we have will be taken away from us (Matt. 25:29). Only as we throw ourselves into slavery to our neighbor do we enjoy the mysterious freedom of God's people, to which we shall turn in the next chapter.

Looked at in a second way, the freedom which we have been given may be seen as the freedom of faith, a freedom to see, to understand, and so to walk as people who have tasted the freedom of the sons of God which we do not yet have, except in this mysterious, anticipatory way. And that is exactly the nature of faith: it is anticipation, an eager waiting, a grasping by hope at that which is not present, not available, not seen. We walk by faith and not by sight, and so to live by faith is not to live by a freedom which we can see, which can be pointed to. It is precisely to live by that to which we cannot point. Yes, and that includes our own faith and our own living by faith: that too is not to be looked at. We walk not by the sight of our own feeble attempts at faithfulness. To walk by faith is to walk with eyes bandaged by our condition of bondage, so that even our own faith is not something to see and lay hold of. All we can grasp is that which grasps us, the strange image of freedom which flashed before our eyes at Easter and then disappeared in the darkness. Insofar as we see at all, then, we see only in part. The freedom of faith is the highly ambiguous, limited freedom to be dimly aware that we have been spoken to in the past and that we will be spoken to again in the future, a future which may come at any moment. So the freedom of faith is an awareness that we are not free: at least we are free to know *that*. And because we hope for freedom, it is a freedom to groan along with the whole of creation, and especially along with creation's Creator, longing for that freedom of the cosmos which is to be unveiled. And in this condition, walking without eyesight, groaning for what is not yet, we are free to walk, to walk in newness of life, in a new if stumbling way.

This freedom, this way of looking at the freedom of the faithful, is also not something which we can have alone. It is something we share, or we lose it. A faith kept to oneself is the talent buried in the ground that the master will take from us (*cf.* Matt. 25:24–29). Faith that is my own possession, my own treasure, turns to rust and dust. Only faith that is shared, only a vision of freedom that is kept busily at work encouraging others to share in that vision, can live. And unless that vision is so exercised to make others rejoice in this hope, it will disappear. Faith is a form of the freedom of man that is under the same law that we have traced out before: it lives corporately shared with others, and it lives for the sake of others, not ourselves, or else it withers and dies.

Finally, we may look briefly at the mystery of freedom in a third form, as the freedom of theology. Christians have always had the freedom to think, to reflect upon what they are to say and do as Christians. We are free to do what we are doing here, to reflect upon the mystery of human freedom. In this third exercise of freedom as well, however, we have not been set free to be isolated by and for ourselves. If we do that, we are not exercising real freedom, and we are not doing theology. Theology is something we do together and for each other, or we don't do it at all. Theology as an aspect of freedom is an event that happens openly and together among us. You can have your private heresy by yourself, but you cannot have your private theology.

In this form too, as theology, our freedom takes the form of service. There is really only one kind of theology that is worthy of the name: responsible theology, theology which is itself a response, which is the result not of our trying to have our own independent thoughts, but of our attempt to make every thought subject to Christ (2 Cor. 10:5). Nor are we left to our own devices to guess when this is the case. The Church can be and is one, holy, and catholic when the Church is also apostolic, when it is the Church in which the apostles, the chosen witnesses to Jesus, have a continuing and lively role in our discussions and reflections. This can happen when we so debate among ourselves, that we are ever attentive to the apostolic writings and especially to the Scriptures which the apostles held to be sacred. Responsible theology happens in that event in which the prophets and the apostles exercise anew their freedom to speak decisively into our discussions, so that in hearing them, the promise of Jesus is fulfilled and we hear also him and the One who sent him (Luke 10:16). It is by sharing in their freedom that we exercise our freedom in Christ to dare to think God's thoughts after him.

3. THE MYSTERY OF ISRAEL'S FREEDOM

We come now to the midpoint of our reflections on the mystery of freedom, and with the name of Israel, we come indeed to the heart of the whole matter before us, to the touchstone of all our reflection. This is the point from which we are able to and must determine whether we are engaged in empty speculation or speaking the truth. For the name of Israel is the control upon all theological reflection that is worth the doing, because in Israel is God heard. Here, in this concrete, human history, in the testimony to these events by prophets and apostles, is where God's freedom is heard of, and thereby heard of as compromised, and therefore heard of as a mystery. Here, therefore, if anywhere, is where the mystery of human freedom has been shown to us.

That is what we have aimed at in the first two chapters. We began with this point and now we have come to the place to open it up with more care. We have spoken of the mystery of revelation, the mystery that by making himself known to certain men, by committing himself to them and binding them to himself (and

that is what made the history of Israel), God has compromised his own freedom, has made his freedom dependent upon that of his creation, thereby making
clear to us that our freedom is bound up with all of
creation. This we have heard within Israel, and within
Israel alone.

Apart from Israel, of course, men have had their ideas
of God and of man. Speculation about God and his
freedom, and about man and human freedom, have
been carried on outside of and without reference to
Israel throughout human history, and it continues to
this day. God has been imagined to be a first cause, a
creative principle, and heavens knows what else. His
freedom has been imagined by some to be absolute and
uncompromised—indeed uncompromisable. On other
occasions by other thinkers, it has been said that God's
freedom is not absolute but the opposite, even nonexist-
ent. Some, indeed many and in every age, have come
to the conclusion that there is no God at all to be free.
Why not? Speculation can surely proceed on its own
way, for when all is said and done, what do we really
know about matters which are presumed to exceed our
understanding?

Likewise, there has been speculation in all ages about
human freedom, ranging from ideas of man as essen-
tially and absolutely free, the Promethean maker of
himself and his destiny, to the theories of those who
have claimed that human freedom is the illusion of an
animal that is but the product of chance and necessity.
Man as pure free spirit, or man as totally determined:
who is to say? A good case can be made on either end
and for many positions in between.

We need to be clear to what extent and in what way
we who claim a part in Israel's heritage are in this same

speculative situation, and in what way or to what degree we are not. It is certain that we no more escape the field of human thought and human language than does anyone else when we speak of divine and human freedom. We can no more transcend the limits of language and thought than can those whom we define as engaging in speculation on such matters. But more than this, we are more limited than others, for we are futher limited by referring to just one line of thinking, one people's talk, namely that which took place in Israel, and which we find laid out for us in the writings of the biblical authors and editors. In those writings we are confronted with Israel's own reflections, her speculations, if you will, upon what had happened to her and what was happening to her, and also upon what she hoped and feared might yet happen to her. Israel's language about God and man, about God's freedom and human freedom, is as surely human language and human reflection as that of any other people. What, then, is so special about Israel?

Now the trouble with this question is that in order to answer it, we must take up a position that already assumes the answer which we give. If we assume that we are not of Israel, we shall be inclined to look at what Israel has had to say as one more expression of people searching for the meaning of human life and history. Asking the question from that position, we may conclude that Israel does present us with interesting features, but we shall have no reason to think that what we hear there is any more binding upon us than what we hear from other sources of human reflection and speculation. On the other hand, if we have heard the voice that Israel has heard, calling us to be heirs and children of Israel, or if we have somehow found persuasive Israel's account of the voice that she has heard, and accept solidarity with her, then we shall probably be convinced that Israel, in its human language, is our model for responding to the one who has spoken. It seems difficult to conceive of any neutral ground on which we could stand that did not already commit us to one answer or the other. There does not appear to be some unbiased position from which we could examine the evidence or hear the argument and decide whether Israel is indeed special (not because of any unique gifts or qualities of Israel, but because here is where God has compromised his freedom and so made himself known in his mystery), or, on the other hand, whether Israel is just one more case of mankind's many attempts to come to terms with reality, doomed, along with all the others, to be classified as unresolvable speculation.

It does not follow from the difficulty of establishing a neutral approach to the question of the special place of Israel in God's purpose, granting that the problem has been identified correctly, that the decision in favor of Israel is an irrational choice. Two arguments are often given for such a judgment. First, it is sometimes said that to accept the singularity of Israel is to turn one's back on the universal for the sake of a particular. The assumption on which this point rests, however, is that the universal and the undifferentiated are always to be preferred to the particular and the definite, which surely begs the question at issue. The particularity and definiteness of human history, of each of our concrete lives, in specific times and places, of actual choices made by actual people, all lend as much or more weight to placing a higher value on particularity in such a matter.

Second, it is sometimes said that for Christians, specifically, there is no reason why there should be any more value or attention given to Israel than to any other theistic or spiritual tradition. But that is to ignore the historical fact that Christianity was born out of and can therefore not define itself apart from Israel. Christians stand unavoidably in a unique historical relationship with Israel, claiming that they are heirs to the promises of Israel's God, children of Abraham by adoption, and that their Lord is Israel's messiah. Surely all these are reasons for the choice for Israel, and if to have coherent reasons for a position is what we mean by being rational, then it seems strange to call such a decision irrational. In such matters, to decide either way is as rational (and as irrational) as to take the alternative course. To call either choice irrational is simply to disapprove of the position so labeled. The choice in such a matter is based on hearing what Israel has to say. It has been the case, down through many centuries, that intelligent, thinking, perfectly reasonable men and women have disagreed, but some of them have heard Israel's voice carrying conviction and have heard through it a voice effectively calling them to come and be part of this people and what has happened to them. To respond by saying yes to this call, on the one hand, and to fail to hear the call at all on the other, are clearly quite different acts, but I see no reason to call either of them irrational.

As a matter of historical fact, it has always been understood within the Church of Jesus Christ, despite its traditional anti-Judaism, that Israel is a people whose history is not like that of any other people, for the single reason that it is in the history of this people that God has compromised his own freedom and consequently has compromised the freedom of this people. They are a people, and if we are with Israel, then we are a people whose understanding of reality, of God and man, is rooted in that event in which it was said: I shall be your God, and you shall be my people. That may indeed have spelled the end of God's freedom as absolute freedom, and it surely spelled the end of Israel's freedom as absolute freedom, but it was Israel's birth, her creation.

Israel was the creation of an act of liberation: to the question of who they were and why they were what they were, Israel's classic answer was this: "We were Pharaoh's slaves in Egypt and the Lord brought us out of Egypt with a mighty hand!"[1] Slaves set free! That is the beginning of this people, and in the light of that happening (the Exodus, they called it), they interpreted their whole past and even the very creation of the world. *Ex tenebris, Lux! Creatio ex nihilo!* That's what they were, and so they understood the world—a gift of sheer grace, the creation of One who by his word made them a people out of nothing: I shall be your God and you shall be my people. And it was so.

Slaves set free. And yet that is not really what happened. Israel's exodus was not the first nor the last time in human history in which slaves have been emancipated only to find their new freedom a condition

[1]Deut. 6:21, part of the reading for the Passover Seder. The rabbinical tradition in Judaism had less interest than had Israel's prophets or much of the Christian tradition in the historical liberation from Egypt. For the rabbis, the liberating event centered rather in the gift of Torah (Law): "When Torah came into the world, freedom came into the world." (Montefiore & Loewe, *A Rabbinic Anthology,* p. 128.) Just as Christians concerned to understand Judaism need to ponder this view of the Law, so well expressed in Psalm 119, so Jews might consider whether the rabbis understood Deut. 6:21 as an answer to the question about the *meaning* of Torah in the preceeding verse.

worse than their old servitude. Escape from slavery, if that is what freedom amounted to, began to look like freedom to die in the desert. The Jews had to discover that their liberation was of a more complex sort than that. They were set free, not to do as they chose or to go where they would, but to be the slaves of the One who had emancipated them. This is the meaning of the Sinai event and the giving of Torah, so central to Israel's history. They were set free to be the people of their Liberator. The strange character of Israel's freedom is what we now have to understand, and it may help in our reflections on the mystery of Israel's freedom if we look at it from several angles or see it under different aspects.

Another and later Israelite put the matter in a way which shows how well he understood that strange exodus: "For freedom," he wrote, "Christ has set us free." Or to put it in the earlier terms and context, Israel was set free from slavery in Egypt for the sake of freedom, in order that freedom might come to be. This means first of all that freedom for Israel was not something possessed; it was something to be aimed for, to long for and to hope for. Israel was set free to be on the way toward freedom. That is the first aspect of the matter which we shall want to consider. But then, following out of this, we need to see that this condition of being aimed at freedom, being destined for freedom, meant for Israel to be the witness to freedom, and that in two senses. So the second aspect of this matter to which we shall attend is Israel's calling to announce freedom, to be the prophet and messenger of freedom. And the third aspect calling for our reflection is that Israel realized that to announce freedom could not be a matter simply of saying something, but rather required doing something: she had to practice freedom, to act out this goal which she did not yet possess. She had to explore how one practices freedom before one has it. When we have considered these matters I think we shall be able to see that the real mystery of Israel's freedom was that she was not, is not, and will not be free apart from the Gentiles. Indeed it was with our eye upon this mystery that we were able to say that the mystery of God's freedom is that he is not and will not be free apart from us, and that the mystery of human freedom is that we cannot have it apart from the rest of humanity. These are nothing more than corollaries of the central mystery, that Israel is to go free only with the liberation of the Gentiles.

Before going further, it would be well to make as clear and as concrete for ourselves as we can to whom we refer when we say "Israel." That was the new name given to Jacob, Abraham's grandson, according to the tradition (Gen. 32:28). That was the name, therefore, under which the twelve tribes carried on, going down into Egypt, and then out under Moses and back to their land of promise. Under that name the people of God's plan and purpose were addressed innumerable times by the prophets. To Israel, as St. Paul put it, belongs "the sonship, the glory, the covenants, the giving of the law, the worship and the promises" (Rom. 9:4). And let us not forget to add that Israel is also now the name of a small, new nation state at the eastern end of the Mediterranean Sea, situated on the land promised to Abraham and his heirs.

Who, then, are the Gentiles? The Gentiles are all the others, all the rest of us, but the rest of us divided into two parts: there are those Gentiles who understand themselves to have become adopted children of Israel, grafted into that tree; and then there are the many more Gentiles who have not accepted such an adoption. Israel marks out one family, with its natural sons and daughters, the Jews, and also its adopted sons and daughters; and then there are all the other families of man. Most of us who call ourselves Christians (although that is but to take on a name presumably coined by unbelievers [Acts. 11:26]) are Israelites only by adoption, Gentiles grafted into a trunk and feeding off roots that are those of Israel by birth.

What is utterly misleading in this matter is a historically absurd expression which was coined less than a century ago and which has become widespread only relatively recently: "the Judaeo-Christian tradition." A critical examination of the historical evidence exposes the fact that whatever might have produced such a tradition was snuffed out, stamped upon, and buried underground early in the Christian era.[2] Instead, what developed was a pagan-Christian tradition, its great feast days celebrated with pagan emblems of fir trees, holly and ivy, and the fertility symbols of eggs and rabbits; its structure and organization modeled on and developing out of the pagan imperial structure; its language and conceptual categories taken over almost unchanged from the pagan world in which it grew. And then, alongside the increasingly powerful pagan-Christian tradition, a smaller, virile, but increasingly defensive Jewish tradition, progressively forced to redefine itself in self-defense before the increasingly venomous and violent explicit anti-Judaism of the pagan-Christian majority. It is as heirs of this development, I submit, and

[2]See Rosemary Ruether, *Faith and Fratricide*, New York, 1974, chapters 3 and 4.

not of a mythical Judaeo-Christian tradition, that we have to reconsider recent history and pick up the pieces of what has happened to Israel, divided into two parodies of itself: a Christianity that has forgotten its forefathers' family name, and a Judaism pressured into an involuntary isolationism.

Not only do we have to be more honest and accurate about what has gone on during the past nineteen centuries, but we especially have to get clear about what has gone on in this last half-century. For we Gentile Christians, with our roots sunk deep into Europe's pagan tradition, are now aware that when we speak of Israel, we speak of different roots, which for centuries we have denied and in our own century have tried to wipe out. The final fruit of our pagan-Christian tradition was the Holocaust, the "final solution" of mostly baptized pagans to annihilate the natural heirs of Israel. If we have any part in God's mysterious promise to Israel, then we depend on those very roots that we have tried to destroy. Apostasy on such a scale, permeating just about the whole of Christendom from top to bottom and from left to right,[3] is a matter of such seriousness that we shall have to reflect on its origins with the greatest care in our last chapter. For it seems safe to assume that when things go so fundamentally wrong, there must have been something seriously sick about Christianity from its earliest days, a sickness which Judaism was quick to detect and point out, but which arrogance, conceit and self-interest prevented Christian ears from hearing.[4] To that most interesting problem we shall

[3]See Franklin Littell, *The Crucifixion of the Jews,* N.Y., 1975.
[4]It might occur to some to try to dismiss this judgment as the expression of an overwrought sense of guilt. Such a response, however, would suffer from two weaknesses. First, it rests on a confusion of the psychological notion of

return. Here we need only make it clear that when we speak of Israel, we speak of the only roots which any of God's people have, be it by birth or by adoption, be it by circumcision or by baptism, the only grounds that any person can claim for having any part in the promises of God. When we speak further about the mystery of Israel's freedom, then, we speak of the mystery of the freedom into which we have been called, be we Jew or Greek, male or female, bond or free. The subject is not about those others and back then: it is about you and me, here and now.

"Hear, O Israel, the Lord our God is one. We were Pharaoh's slaves in Egypt and the Lord brought us out of Egypt with a mighty hand!" Israel's story, our story if we can hear it as such, is one that begins in an act of liberation. We are those who have been set free. But what a strange freedom this is! Israel was loosed from Pharaoh's bitter yoke to do what? To wander in hunger and thirst in the desert! Is there not something profoundly ambiguous about the freedom of Israel? Out of slavery into the hostile environment of the Sinai desert. After freedom comes hardship. And see how that same pattern repeats itself again and again, as if Israel's Lord were trying to drive home a lesson hard to learn. (Judging by Christianity's flight from its Israelitic roots to cling rather to the comforting trunk of paganism, it is

---

guilt with the legal notion of a relationship of responsibility. The judgment made above refers to the well-documented relationship between the anti-Judaism of the Christian tradition and the modern "anti-Semitism" that came to a head in Hitler's Germany. Reference is to the historical records, not to how anyone may feel about them. Second, and more important, the response misses the point that, regardless of responsibility, its traditional anti-Judaism places Christianity in the self-contradictory position of denying that in terms of which it must define itself.

a lesson which we seem not to want to learn.) Freedom was not something to be possessed, but rather something to be longed for. When Israel was delivered from the danger of enemy attacks, so runs the repetitive cycle of the Book of Judges, it was always to fall back again into insecurity. And when prosperity and national security seemed surely to have triumphed in the Davidic Kingdom, they would only lead to the long decline toward invasions by Assyria, the destruction of Jerusalem as well as of the whole Northern Kingdom, and the captivity in Babylon. Again there was deliverance for the captives, a liberation and the time of the Second Temple, only to be followed by bondage in the occupied territory of the Greeks and then the Romans. Are we not witnesses today to a further repetition of the lesson, when, after the worst oppression by far, the new liberation, in the form of the state of Israel, is turning out not to be a deliverance into joy and peace, but the way into danger, insecurity and a steady diet of wars and rumors of wars? One might think that, as the prophets told us plainly enough on more than one occasion, somebody is trying to say something to us.

What is being said now is what the prophets heard long since: Israel's freedom is the freedom to long for freedom, to have its heart and imagination kindled to agonize for freedom as no other people has agonized. They were set free, they have been again and again set free *for* freedom. And that means, clearly, not to possess freedom as their own treasure, to enjoy for themselves, but rather to have real freedom always and only as an anticipatory hint, in order that mankind's freedom, the earth's freedom, and, yes, God's freedom might be Israel's consuming passion. Israel's call, like Abraham's, was and is to be a pilgrim people, on the way, not having attained, but pointing on ahead toward something better, a strange finger piercing the curtain of the future, feeling out and working for that which is not yet. What a contrast between Israel's calling and path, and that of those who presume to speak of blessed assurance! No, for Israel, it has always been the fear and trembling of Abraham on the way to Mount Moriah, of Moses in the wilderness of Sinai, of Jesus in Gethsemene, and of the author of those strange words, "work out your own salvation with fear and trembling, for God is at work in you" (Phil. 2:12), the apostle Paul. It is part of the mystery of Israel's freedom that Israel has never possessed freedom, has only glimpsed it, has been steadily and terribly drawn on by it. Indeed, freedom is Israel's *goal,* not a possession.

This brings us, then, to the second step of the development of our subject. If Israel is set free for freedom, not to have freedom, what is the meaning of that "for"? Can we further determine this strange relationship between Israel and its freedom? We can do so with the help of a word that needs careful definition because of its widespread misuse. The word for Israel's relation to freedom is "witness." Israel is called to be a witness to freedom.

To be a witness is, whether one likes it or not, to be in a position to tell the truth. It is, pleasant or unpleasant as may be the prospect, to be in a position to report on certain events. The witness has the right, the authority, and the obligation to speak up on the matter in question. We have had enough cases in our society in recent years of persons who could in fact have been witnesses, but who have preferred to remain silent. We have had witnesses in Vietnam, in the State Department, in the CIA, the FBI, the Committee to Reelect

the President. Most have preferred silence and ano-
nymity. So have many who have seen what was going
on in IBM, GM, ITT, and many another center of
power. Some have been witnesses of death by stabbing
of persons on the streets of New York and other cities.
One may have found oneself in the position of being a
witness, and have found, as many have before, that
there is much to be said for *not* being a witness. To be
a witness is to risk your very self. Since the issue of the
rationality of faith has been raised before, it may be
admitted candidly: no rational person, as the Enlight-
enment has defined rationality for us all, would choose
to be a witness.

But Israel has been called to be a witness, and a witness to a freedom which she has only glimpsed but does
not have. That means woe is Israel's lot, that she is called
to announce that which does not exist, a calling doomed
to derision. She is not called to announce something
which is there, plain for any person to see. She is not
called to point to herself as possessing that for which all
persons long. She is called to announce something
which does not exist, and woe to her, ten times over, if
she announce it as something which she pretends is in
fact present.

To be called to be a witness, as Israel has been, is to
be commissioned as a herald. That is a definite and
specific commission. It fixes Israel's identity and purpose. A herald's task is to deliver a message, to say what
he has been commissioned to say. The herald may have
his own opinions. He may develop a philosophy of life.
He may even have interesting theories about the one
who has sent him. None of that, however, is part of his
job. His job is to deliver the message with which he has
been entrusted to those to whom he has been sent.

Least of all is he supposed to tell about himself, his interesting inner experiences or feelings. No, he is simply a messenger. And the message is to announce God's freedom, delivery for the captives, healing for the sick, sight for the blind. The message, in sum, is that the One who sent the messenger intends, wills and longs for the freedom of every man, woman, and child. The herald exists for the sake of these others. He exists to get the word through to them that freedom is decisive, that liberation is what this whole world is about.

Israel's particular call, however, was to be the witness of specific events. When in the course of a case at law, we need to find out some general principles, be they of law, ballistics, or psychology, then we call in some expert for advice. Perhaps from them we shall get some eternal principles or self-evident truths. But from the witness we want to hear only what he or she has seen. What happened? That is the only proper question for the witness. And if the witness wanders off into talk of eternal principles or self-evident truths, then we do well to dismiss such remarks as immaterial and irrelevant.

Since Israel has been called to be a witness, the only matters of which Israel is authorized to speak are accounts of events. What Israel has to say about freedom, then, must always and only refer to actual, particular happenings, as for example, to a particular group of slaves who escaped from Egypt, to a Law received at Sinai, to a concrete group of captives in Babylon who came back to Jerusalem, to a Temple rebuilt in that city,[5] or to a certain Israelite from Nazareth who was

---

[5]Rabbi Joshua ben Levi said: "If the nations had known how valuable the Temple was for them, they would have surrounded it with forts in order to

tortured to death and yet appeared to his friends after three days. These are the events, the concrete cases of God's mysterious liberating power which Israel is authorized to report. And if God is the God of the living, not just of the dead, then why should Israel not go on and tell of other events in this same history, up to and including the mysterious revitalization of Judaism and the founding of the state of Israel after the horror of the Holocaust? The Exodus after Egypt, Jerusalem after Babylon, Easter after the cross, and Israel after Auschwitz: must not the witness just lay this before the world, to find out if the world can see the single line that runs through them all? The evidence is ambiguous, no doubt. But Israel is not called upon to be the judge or jury. Its calling is simply to be the witness, to see to it that these events are not lost sight of, not distorted, not turned into eternal truths or universal principles.

This leads us to note, then, the prophetic aspect of Israel's commission to be God's witness in the world, the light for the nations. Because Israel is witness to this line of events in its own history, it must dare to call attention to events in the history of others that look like yet more circumstantial evidence that God is a God of freedom and longs for the liberation of all men. She may not be commissioned to bear witness to these events with the same assurance as those of which she is commanded to speak, but she can hardly ignore them altogether. She will notice the emergence of a new

---

protect it. It was even more valuable to them than to the Israelites, for Solomon in his prayer of dedication said, 'And concerning the foreigner ... do according to all that the foreigner calls to thee to do' (1 Kings 8:41–43), but when he touches on the Israelites, he says, 'Render unto everyone according to his ways,' that is, give to him what he asks if it is fitting for him, and if it is not fitting, give it not." Cited in *A Rabbinic Anthology,* p. 115.

Cuba, freed from the tyranny, torture, corruption and poverty of its former regime in our own days, or the yet more fantastic rise of a new China out of centuries of poverty and corruption. When even so sober an observer as James Reston of the *New York Times* detects taking place in China today a very remaking of the moral fabric of the people, the children of Israel will surely want to whisper about these matters to each other and maybe drop hints about them out loud. Can they not be signs that the God of freedom, no matter how mysteriously compromised his freedom may be, still works together with mankind toward his goal, toward that acceptable year of the Lord when the whole creation will be free? Could these movements toward political and economic freedom be part of his plan?

At this point, Israel must be careful—not cautious or nervous, but careful—for it is called to discriminate carefully between those events which are said to be steps to freedom, but which contradict Israel's witness, and those events which are said to be steps to freedom and agree with its witness. For whenever anything happens, no matter what, there will always be someone who will call it a step to freedom. The bombing of Cambodia and the fall of the Lon Nol government were both called steps to freedom. Clearly, at least one of them was not, and possibly neither was. It is Israel's difficult and painful burden to have to make up its mind in such cases. For a witness must tell not only nothing but the truth, but also the whole truth.

There has been much misunderstanding about Israel's task and purpose due to a voluntaristic misreading of our commission. When according to the apostolic writing (Acts 1:8) Jesus told his disciples, "You will be my witnesses," he wasn't giving them advice, or recommending a course of action for them to follow. He was simply telling them what had happened to them and therefore what was going to happen to them. Israel's commission to be a witness is just that: whether Israel likes it or not, and it has usually not liked it, it has just turned out to be the case that Israel is a witness to the world. Witnessing is something that happens to you, not something you do. There is, as it were, almost an inevitability to it. If we Gentile Israelites-by-adoption want to understand this, we can do no better than follow Paul's order, which works here as elsewhere: the Jew first, and then the Gentile. So if we would understand the inevitability of witness, we can learn by looking at the Jews. They stand, regardless of what they do or say, whether they want to or not, as God's sign posts, his witnesses. Gentile Christians talk a lot about being "in the world but not of it." That is for them an ideal. For the Jew, however, it is a brute fact. They *are* in the world as a people not of the world, different from the world, a witness to him who called Abraham, spoke to Moses, and gave the Law. From our older brothers, we younger brothers, Gentiles grafted into Israel, still have much to learn.

This brings us to the third aspect of the mystery of Israel's freedom, for this too is something that Gentile converts have been poor at learning from their elder brothers. Israel's calling is to exercise herself in, to take up the practice of, that freedom to which she has been called and does not yet possess. Paradoxical as it must sound, this is Israel's difficult but also joyful task: to experiment with living in a condition that is not yet real, the condition of freedom. How do you do that? Well may it be asked, for we have been instructed: by keeping the Law. All 613 commandments? That is and remains a matter of debate, even among our Jewish brothers. Moses summed it up in just ten, if you can't cope with 613, and Micah got it down to only three: the doing of justice, the loving of mercy, and walking humbly with our God (6:8).[6] And if that is still too complex, then one whom all of Israel acknowledges as a prophet, and some of Israel claim is more than a prophet, worked it down, by selective quotations from the Torah, to just two (Matt. 22:37–39): love God with everything you have (Deut. 6:5), and love your neighbor as your very self (Lev. 19:18).[7] As can be seen, it doesn't really make much difference what the count is. From the 613 down to the two, a path is provided, a lamp to our feet, on this way we are called to walk, practicing the *Shalom,* the peace of God, and doing the righteousness of God, which are the promised conditions of the freedom in store for the whole of creation.

Why then Christianity's traditional disparagement of the Law, as if the Law were against the Gospel, as if the Law were not itself Gospel, good news? Because one Jew, Paul of Tarsus, was upset about how some of his fellow Jews seemed to him to be misusing the Law. And is that a good reason? Any good thing can and will be abused. But because a few forget what the Law is all about and especially forget him who gave it, is that a reason to turn on it as the enemy? By no means. If we are to understand Law, Torah, then we must do more than just worry about its misuse and read more than Epistles to the Galatians and the Romans. No, we must

---

[6] A passage from Rabbi Simlai making the same point, with further examples, is to be found in *A Rabbinic Anthology,* p. 199.

[7] Jesus was hardly the only rabbi to quote this. *Cf. A Rabbinic Anthology,* p. xi.

read Moses, the Pentateuch, the prophets, and all of Scripture. There we see Torah in its mystery, as a practice program for walking in the freedom which has not yet come. Like children pretending to be grown-ups, like prisoners trying to forget they are in jail and pretending that they are free to come and go as they will, so are we called by Torah to practice the freedom of the sons of God in a liberated creation before its time. Is this not good news, that we are allowed to begin right now to exercise ourselves in the righteousness, the mercy and the humble walking which is promised for us in the coming age? So if we take one of the easy steps, such as resisting the non-temptation to boil a kid in its mother's milk, or one of the harder ones, such as resisting the temptation to be unfaithful to our husband or wife, or the attractive one (which our culture leads us to forget) of systematically loafing on the sabbath, then we should rejoice and leap for joy, for we are learning the baby steps of how to walk in the age of the messiah.

Insofar as we of Israel meditate on Torah and live by Torah, we shall be doing something quite concrete and worldly. We shall be solidly in this world. But in doing this, we shall necessarily be doing something other than most do in our culture. We shall be to that extent countercultural and in that sense not of this world, this old age of oppression. And when our neighbors notice and ask why we do such silly things rather than follow the American crowd, when they ask about the odd new habits that we are trying to learn, then we may say, as Israel has always said: "We were pharaoh's slaves in Egypt, and the Lord brought us out of Egypt with a mighty hand!" As the witnesses to the God of liberation, we are destined to be a peculiar people. In an unjust world, we have been set free to practice actual justice.

In an oppressed world, we are free to speak up for the oppressed. Our calling is to show forth God's love and justice and mercy until the day of his messiah. For just this strange task, Israel has been set free.

This brings us to yet another aspect of the mystery of Israel's freedom. A witness cannot carry out his role all by himself. He exists for the sake of those to whom he is sent. As the author of Isaiah 49 put it, It is too light a thing that Israel should be God's servant: God has given Israel to be a light to the nations, that his liberation may reach to the ends of the earth (49:6).

God's plan, in short, seems to be that our practice of Torah is to be used by him to bring the whole of this world to the freedom for which he longs. We are sent, as the author of Matthew says, to make fellow servants of all nations, baptizing them in the name of God, he who shall be whom he shall be, he who also opens himself to men and makes himself known, he who further opens men to respond to him and walk in his way (28:19).

Now an odd thing happened on the way from Sinai to the present. In the fullness of time, at the moment that seemed right to him, God awakened a strange new movement among his people, of which we shall have more to say in the last chapter (especially about the strange events of its beginning, which have been even more strangely misunderstood). The result of this new movement was that some of God's people, Israel, the Jews, felt compelled to acknowledge that God was in the act of expanding the family of Israel. He was adding Gentiles to Judaism, from Gentile stones raising up children to Abraham!

Jews of that time were of two minds about this new development. Some saw this new movement, which began admitting Gentiles into Israel, as a dangerous compromise, a betrayal of Israel's calling to be a lamp set on a stand, and so distinct and different from all that surrounded that lamp. Other Jews argued rather that this new movement was God's doing and the fulfillment of Israel's calling to be a light that in fact enlightened the world. That debate still goes on, between those whom the world knows as the Jews, and those whom the world first gave the name, and continues to call, the Christians. We should never forget, however, that the difference began, as it should have remained, as a family argument among Jews over the mystery of Israel's freedom.

One of the most interesting fragments of that debate, which comes down to us from the time when this family quarrel was being developed, is contained in the eleventh chapter of the letter of Paul to the Israelites in Rome. Chapters 9 through 11 reflect Paul's agony over this quarrel, that it had burst into the open, and that not all Jews could come to an agreement in the matter. And at the end of that section, speaking to the new Gentile Israelites about those Jews who felt that this opening to the Gentiles was a mistake, he came to the following conclusion. Of them, those Jews who disagreed with him, Paul said: As regards the good news of this new development, they are enemies of God, for *your* sake (11:28). That is, had they agreed with Paul that the life and proclamation of Jesus, and especially the strange double-ending of that life, signaled a new stage in Israel's history, then this turn toward the Gentiles might never have been made. I find the reasoning obscure here, but Paul's reasoning seldom fits our western canons of logic. Perhaps his idea was that if the disciples of Jesus had met sufficient acceptance among their fellow

Jews, they would have had no time or inclination to find other listeners. Paul may have been doing a bit of market analysis here, pointing out that a second market for the gospel only opened up because the first sales campaign was something of a failure. In any case, his first point is clear: the one sense in which the Jews can be faulted for rejecting the gospel is that this was God's way of getting the message to the Gentiles, which is hardly much of a criticism.

To make clear that the fault is not serious, Paul continued: "But as regards election, they are beloved for the sake of their forefathers. For the gifts and the call of God are irrevocable." Paul intended to leave no doubt in his readers' minds: the Jews are God's irrevocably chosen people, his prime instrument for the liberation of his creation. They remain Abraham's heirs forever, no matter how well or poorly they follow in Abraham's path. It is a matter of God's mysterious freedom, not of human choice.

And therefore, the fact that some of the Jews, even the vast majority, would not follow God's new lead in the events surrounding Jesus of Nazareth, the fact that most of them could not call Jesus the Messiah, by no means takes from them their central role of being the witnesses of God's longing and working for the liberation of creation. "Just as you were once disobedient to God and now have received mercy because of their disobedience," Paul continued (Rom. 11:30–31), addressing his Gentile readers, "so they have now been disobedient in order that by the mercy shown to you they also may receive mercy." Gentile membership in Israel, in other words, is the merciful result of the Jewish rejection of the disciples' message about Jesus, and now that their rejection has had that result, they will be treated with exactly that same mercy which was shown to pagan Gentiles. That does *not* mean that they will stop being Jews and become Christians. Nothing could have been further from Paul's mind than the inexcusable idea of the later theologians and Church that Christianity was supposed to displace Judaism. On the contrary, Paul had just before this reminded his readers that they, as Gentiles, had been as a wild olive branch grafted onto a cultivated olive tree, Israel (v. 17). If the Jews, in their rejection of what God had done in Jesus could be compared to branches being broken off the trunk, then, Paul said, it was to be expected that these natural branches would be grafted back onto *their own* olive tree (v. 24). Onto their own olive tree, he said, as natural branches. He did not even hint at the idea that they would have to be converted into wild branches first.[8] No, Israel for Paul was now to move forward in a new dual way. At the center, as they had been from the first, would be the Jews, the people of Abraham's descent and promise, this quite particular people. As ever, you may be a Jew by birth, or you may become a Jew, a proselyte, a convert, by identifying yourself with this people and taking up their burden as your own. The Jews are not a race and not a religion. They are what God made them, a people with a special role in history, living lights to humanity, if humanity cares to notice, given over to the worship of the Creator of this world and the One who wills its liberation. But now there is to be an appendage to Judaism, which unhappily came to be called Christianity. These people are to act as emissaries, as ambassadors, calling the world to

[8]For a contrary but unsupported reading, see Ruether, *Faith and Fratricide,* p. 106.

worship the God of the Jews and to serve the liberation of the world as that God has defined liberation.[9]

We could use another figure and say that, as Paul presented it, Judaism is the white hot filament of Israel's light to the nations, and the Christians are to be the Fresnel lens to spread the rays of that light out upon the world.[10] Without the lens, the light will not reach as far, but without the central filament, there will be no light at all. Together, they make up the one Israel of God, his co-workers for the liberation of his creation.

It is hardly news to say that, obviously, something went wrong with God's plan, assuming that Paul had it anywhere near right. Something went desperately wrong. There was from the first a family quarrel with such Jews as Paul of Tarsus, the Hellenistic Jew named Barnabas, and their fellows on one side, and with such other Jews as Ananias and Tertullus and their fellows on the other, with perhaps a third party to the dispute, including such Jews as James, the brother of Jesus, and Simon who was called Peter. Our sources for this dispute are limited and hardly impartial. That family quarrel among Jews about the true future of Judaism and about the propriety of calling Jesus the Messiah was turned by events into a bitter fight marked by hatred

[9]Since writing this, I was comforted to hear my reading of Romans 11 confirmed by Professor Krister Stendahl in a lecture given at the 1975 annual meeting of the Society for Biblical Literature, in which he called attention to the fact that Paul concludes with a vision of the consummation of God's plan and a doxology in which there is not a single Christological reference! For the opposite and more traditional view, see Gregory Baum, *The Jews and the Gospel*, London, 1961.

[10]At the time these words were written, I had not yet read Franz Rosenzweig's *The Star of Redemption*, Boston, 1971. He had made use of almost exactly this metaphor in Part III of his remarkable book, with Judaism as the fire and Christianity as the rays.

and violence. We shall consider the central issue in the last chapter, but we have in any case to live with the consequences of how things developed. Decisive, surely, was the fact that at least one of the three groups was apparently massacred in the destruction of Jerusalem by the Roman army in 70 C.E. Undoubtedly the elements of human jealousy and pride were important among the Christian sect of Judaism in its competition with a Judaism that proved able to thrive vigorously even with its capital city destroyed and its land controlled by the Roman military-industrial complex. The result was that the wild olive branch began pretending that it was the whole tree, that having been grafted on, it had killed off the old tree and was now its successor. The sacred Scripture of Israel received a new designation: the Old Testament, good only for being read as proof-texts to support the apostolic writings, which became in time a so-called New Testament.

Was it then such a radical departure for much later Christians, under urging from a National Socialist government, to want to throw away that Old Testament altogether, to prove that wild olive branches could be grafted just as well onto the trunk of Nordic mythology and thrive in the blood and soil of Nazi Germany? And so we come down to the final fruits of this perversion of the one history of God's one Israel, made up of the Jews and the Gentile sect called Christians: having murdered six million of God's people, Adolf Hitler died a baptized Catholic, never to this day denied his place on the rolls of his Church, and a similar unchallenged place is held by that good Lutheran Hermann Goering, Hitler's second-in-command.[11] Does it not look as if the

---

[11] Littell, *The Crucifixion of the Jews,* p. 48.

Fresnel lens has blackened to such an extent as to be useless for God's purposes with Israel? Has the wild branch turned out to be a parasitical vine that would choke Israel to death? Under these circumstances, it is difficult to see how we could come to any other conclusion than this: if such a Church were to pretend to talk about a theology of liberation, it would be the final blasphemy. There can be no Christian talk of liberation, of the freedom of God's creation, until Christians. can get down on their knees and crawl, slowly, painfully, and in dead seriousness, back to Judaism and confess that we have sinned against heaven and against these our older brothers, and begin to learn again the mystery of Israel's calling.[12]

These reflections are by no means intended to encourage Christians to convert to Judaism. That would violate the integrity of Judaism. We have no reason to think that that is what God has planned for Christians, nor are we given such a lead by the apostolic writings. Moreover, Judaism is what it is today partly as a result of what Christians and ex-Christians have done to it, over and above killing a third of the Jews in cold blood. Long before it came to that atrocity, we, or our forefathers in the Church, set up such a barrage of scorn, hatred and vilification, that it led in time to persecutions and pogroms of which Hitler's was only the capstone, that we have forced Judaism into a defensiveness and ingrown protectiveness that have hardly been ideally suited to Israel's task. Those traits did accomplish the one thing necessary: Judaism's survival. But how

[12]I would recall footnote 4 of this chapter. Guilt *feelings* or a guilt *complex* are not the issue. What is at stake is the integrity of Christianity as a potential agent of God's purposes for the liberation of his creation.

Judaism might look, with Christianity as its lens or branch rather than its persecutor, we do not yet know. What we can count on is that until this relationship is restored to its proper form, Israel's potentially liberating light will not shine in this dark age.

If that light does not shine, if the darkness continues to get darker, as it certainly appears to be doing, then we can forget about Israel's freedom. For God's plan for Israel from the beginning, as was clear in the promise to father Abraham, is not for Israel's sake, but for the sake of the whole creation. If there is to be freedom for Israel, it will come with the freedom for the nations, the Gentiles, baptized and unbaptized. Apart from the nations, apart from the whole creation, Israel, both Judaism and its Christian branch, can only have tiny sips of liberation, little anticipations to entice it to long for and work for the liberation which God wills for all of this earth. Whether the Synagogue will ever come to acknowledge the Church as her legitimate if adopted daughter, I do not know. If the daughter would stop acting as if she had displaced the mother and had become the second bride of her father, it would certainly help.[13] The Jews have accused themselves of a good bit of playing the harlot in their day, but that is no match for this incestuous Electra-fixation which Christianity has elevated into high doctrine. The mystery of Israel's freedom is that it is bound up with that of the Gentiles. But there will be no freedom for the nations and for creation until Israel's light shines again, and that in turn awaits the day when this family quarrel is once more

[13]The mother-daughter metaphor was suggested by Jehuda Halevi in his *Kuzari* (IV, 23) and developed by Rosenzweig in *The Star of Redemption*. It has lacked a climate favorable to growth.

returned to the intimacy of the family rather than being exposed to public view. If any Christians care at all for the liberation of the oppressed and for the liberation from the bondage of decay in which Paul saw all of creation caught, they will make their way back to the synagogue, hat in hand so to speak, if not crawling on their knees, to begin to get matters straightened out within the very household of God. Only after that can we look forward to the unfolding of the mystery of Israel's freedom, only a few of the aspects of which we have been considering.

4. THE MYSTERY
OF EASTER

We now arrive at the issue which painfully split Israel into Synagogue and Church, stunted the trunk and warped the branch of the one history of God's one people. At the same time, however, we have reached that which was the occasion for us Gentiles having any room in Israel's house, and the ground for any possible talk about freedom as a Christian goal. I refer, of course, to the center and starting point of Christianity: Easter, the resurrection of Jesus from the dead, his designation as God's annointed or messiah. Jesus of Nazareth, King of the Jews: so he was charged, mockingly, by his Roman executioners. What happened on Easter confirmed that they had written truer than they knew. Whatever it was that happened on that day and the days following, together with the way in which it was understood, is what stands between the Synagogue and the Church, but it accounts for us Gentiles having a part in Israel's history and it forms the rock foundation for our speaking of freedom as a Christian goal.

As a stimulus to critical reflection, I am going to argue that the Church has misinterpreted its foundation, that it has on the whole misread the apostolic witness to Easter, and that it has consequently misrepresented the Messiahship of Jesus.[1] The consequences, I shall argue, have been to set Israel at war with itself, to put Christianity on the side of the oppressors far more often than on the side of the oppressed, and to make real freedom as a serious goal the last thing which the world has come to expect of Christians. In the course of my argument, I hope also to make clear that by properly listening to the apostles and to the other voices of Israel, we may freely make a fresh start, that we may become free for the service of creation's freedom, as a goal to be pursued without restraint. By the end I intend to have made clearer how the mystery of freedom— God's, creation's, and Israel's—is all caught up, unified and revealed in the central mystery of Easter, and it is just this mystery which the doctrine of the Trinity, properly understood, can be seen to express.

Let us begin by asking what happened on Easter. Already we are in trouble with our question, for there is more than one sense in which something may be said to have happened. Let us suppose, then, that we ask what happened on Easter first as critical historians. The oldest written records we have are copies of a letter that was penned some twenty years after Easter and

---

[1]That the apostolic writings are open to such a misreading can hardly be denied; they are full of the polemics typical of a bitter family fight. A Gentile reader of those writings, however, is liable to forget that familial context. Rosemary Ruether is not altogether wrong when she presents the "New Testament" and its sayings against "the Jews" as evidence that the glass is half empty *(Faith and Fratricide)*. Seen from another angle, however, as our discussion of Romans 11 in the last chapter indicates, the same glass can be seen to be half full. It is sobering to reflect that nineteen centuries of Christian commentary on the apostolic writings have gone by with so little provided to help us decide what is right in this matter!

appeals to an oral tradition evidently well fixed by that time (1 Cor. 15:1 ff). According to that tradition, Jesus appeared to his disciples on several occasions after his death. The oral tradition also said that God raised Jesus from the dead, and it added that according to the Scriptures, God did this on the third day after Jesus had died.

Copies of writings another twenty years later (the Gospel of Mark) add evidence of an oral tradition that this act of God had taken place at least by the third day, that is by Easter, the first day of the week after the celebration of the Passover. They offer further evidence of another old oral tradition that on that day it was discovered that the tomb in which Jesus had been buried was empty. So far as we know, there is nothing in even the oldest strata of the oral tradition about anyone having seen this event, and so no clear evidence that it did in fact take place on the first day of the week. What is clear is that that day was from the first assumed to have been the day of this event.

Perhaps it should be pointed out that according to the logic of this oral tradition, the story of an empty tomb is presented as a consequence of the story of Jesus having been raised. The argument, that is to say, was not that the tomb was empty and that therefore Jesus had been raised. It was rather that Jesus had been raised, and therefore the tomb was empty. More importantly, it should be noticed that the tradition is emphatic that Jesus was raised by God, not that he raised himself (Acts 2:24, 32; 3:15; 4:10; Rom. 4:24; 6:4; 1 Cor. 15:4, 15; Phil. 2:9, 32; etc.). To claim that Jesus was able to raise himself is not only contrary to the tradition, it also smacks of that denial of his genuine humanity and the reality of his death that was one of the earliest misunderstandings of the tradition which the young

Church had to resist. It is comparable to saying that Jesus must have known that the United States would lose in Vietnam, because he knew everything, being divine. But that sort of divinity which is unaffected by time and place is not the divinity of the God of Israel. That is a concept of divinity based on some other deity, some pagan deity whose freedom is not compromised by genuine creation and by binding himself to a particular people. That sort of pagan divinity may be utterly above history and have a freedom which is absolute and unqualified. The divinity with which this oral tradition dealt, however, is of another sort. It is a divinity that poured itself out in the human history of this man from Nazareth, whose death was real. When the story speaks of him as having been raised, the power was not in that dead corpse, but in the One whom that dead man had called Father.[2]

On the level of history, that is, as far as historical research will take us, we find a group of people saying and believing that God had raised Jesus from the dead. But how could we know, as historians, what that means? The accounts coming from that oral tradition do not make this at all clear. It was not, apparently, a case of resuscitation, as if the heart began again to beat, the blood to flow, the lungs to breathe. Then we would have had a strange medical case of a body having ceased to function for a minimum of about five to a maximum of about thirty-eight hours (we don't know how long an interval it was within the limits of sundown on Friday to sunrise on Easter) and then having begun to function again. But that is not what the record sup-

[2]See Montefiore and Loewe, *A Rabbinic Anthology*, pp. 16, 62, 64, 66, 71, *passim*, for many examples of this form of address by other rabbis.

ports. For the tradition says he appeared, and then disappeared. He came to his disciples, we are told, but then he either could not or would not stay with them, and the former seems strongly suggested (*e.g.*, Luke 24:31). He was not to be touched, one story says (John 20:17). He appeared in a room with the doors locked (John 20:19). He ate fish with his disciples, we are told, and yet there was a real problem of recognition (Luke 24:36–43). The temptation to take the appearances as those of some sort of ghost was evidently strong, and in each case recognition was far from instantaneous, even for those who had been closest to him.

A person, as we use the concept, is always embodied. Was what appeared to the disciples something that we would call a body? Bodies don't appear and disappear like that. Paul suggests the term "spiritual body," as opposed to a terrestrial body, but that just gives us another way of saying that we don't have any term for this strange variation on embodiment. And yet, the tradition is insistent that it was Jesus himself, the crucified one, who appeared and was now alive, in some new, strange sense of the word. For this man, who had been executed by the Romans only a few days before, death was not the last word, not the end of his story. To say that, however, is simply to admit that we cannot understand what happened there on the level of historical inquiry.

Our historical perplexity must remain, but there is nevertheless another level on which we can approach the question of what happened on Easter. We can and should ask ourselves what we shall make of this. The "this" is the tradition which lies behind and is reflected in the apostolic writings. The "this" includes even more centrally but less understandably, the strange "whatever-it-was" that caused the disciples to speak as they did. The question of what we make of this, the question for faith, is whether God was saying something to us in this strange happening. After death, a new beginning, however ambiguous and unsatisfactory: is that what was being said? In which case, if memory has not failed us utterly, we may recall having heard something similar before; there is something vaguely familiar in that voice! Remember how slavery was followed by that ambiguous freedom to wander in the wilderness? And now, remember the events of our own century, how the Holocaust, the mass murder of six million men, women, and children of Israel, was followed by that ambiguous new phenomenon, the return of a remnant to the land of promise, the birth of the new state of Israel, immediately to be locked into the fate of any nation state, caught in the ambiguities of power politics, living almost constantly with wars and the rumor of wars. Do not these events betray a common hand? Can we not hear in each of them the same voice? What was said in the days of Moses and has been said in our own century was said also in that first century of our common era; namely, that evil, oppression, torture and death are real, all too real, but that they are not the last reality. The last reality is goodness, freedom, righteousness, liberation and life. Because that is what Easter was about, as that is what the Exodus was about, and also as that is what the Return is about, we may know that that is what God is about!

We celebrate this event on the first day of every week. That is the first day of Creation, of God's work, and so the first day of our work week. We do not celebrate it on the Sabbath, the day of God's rest and so of human rest. Saturday is the day of rest for God and man, but Sunday, the first day of the week, is the day of God's creative work, and also the day of this strange work of God. But shall we call it the first day of God's new creation? The Church has usually thought so and celebrated Easter as the day of victory. But was it a victory? Or have we here something just as ambiguous as the Exodus into the desert and the birth of the state of Israel into a condition of repeated wars, something so ambiguous that we might better say that it is not yet clear that it was a victory?

In one sense, according to the claim of the apostles, Easter was, at least for Jesus of Nazareth, a victory over the tyranny of the past tense: he *is* alive, in the present, they proclaimed. God did something for Jesus not done for any other man, causing his history, his story, to resume after his death, and not merely as any man's story may continue in the memory of those who live on. To this man it was said that death was not the last word. In another sense, however, his was a victory so qualified as to make one wonder. He was alive, but what sort of victory was it that could not be realized in a full and open return to the land of the living? He could appear, but he could not stay. His disciples called him Lord, but the kingship of death and oppression continued as before. Indeed he instilled hope and courage in his friends, but is that all he had hoped for himself?

Jesus came proclaiming that the reign of God was at hand, that people should turn around the direction of their lives in preparation for this new era. "The reign of God" is an expression something like "the reign of Queen Elizabeth III," as we have suggested. It refers not to a place, but to a new period of history. The reign of Queen Victoria can be dated. We don't know when (or if) the reign of Queen Elizabeth III will begin, nor how long it will last. And we have been given no indications of what it will be like in the time of Elizabeth III. Jesus proclaimed that the reign of God was just about to begin, and that it would go on forever. He came as the advance herald of this new age, himself the sign that it was about to begin. It would certainly come within the lifetime of some of his hearers, he said. His disciples would not have covered the tiny province of Judea with the news before it arrived. When he ate supper with his friends, the night he was arrested by the Romans, he said that the next time they drank together, the new age would have already begun.

He also had much to say about what to expect upon the arrival of the new age, which would be like a revolution of fantastic dimensions, and about what could be expected once it had begun. It would be a time of righteousness and peace. There would be no more war and oppression. Sickness and disease would be done away, and even death would have no place on earth. In parable after parable, he suggested how it would be in that time.

Now in all honesty, with our older brothers in Israel, the Jews, listening from around the corner, compare all that, so faithful to the messianic hopes of Israel, with the meager consequences of Easter. Only in the single case of Jesus himself, and that in a way so ambiguous as to be baffling, was there any triumph over the conditions of the old age. His followers received a downpayment, as Paul put it, the gift of the Spirit, which consisted primarily in an agonized longing for the great day that had been promised. A tiny flock of eager and longing disciples was all there was to show for Easter, firm in hope, rejoicing in a few individual healings, some changes in life-style, and also some cases of glossolalia, but just as firmly at the mercy of the forces of oppression, tyranny and death as people had ever been. Is that the great victory that Christendom celebrates? Or was that the great deception with which Judaism has taunted its Christian tormentors? Or could it be that both of these interpretations have missed the point?

This brings us to perhaps the strangest of all the developments that have taken place in the history of that incestuous daughter of Judaism, the Christian Church. Sometime toward the end of the first century or early in the second, probably before the movement was a hundred years old, there was set in motion a tremendous cover-up. The cover-up has worked so well that the plain evidence lies right under our eyes and no one seems to be able to see it anymore. Read with fresh eyes, the writings of the apostolic community (ordinarily printed under the title, *The New Testament*) provide ample evidence of the fact that the early Christians were in genuine agony. Jesus had predicted that the new era, the reign of God, usually translated misleadingly as the "Kingdom" of God, would begin immediately, and it had not yet started. What had gone wrong? Why didn't Messiah appear and inaugurate the promised messianic age? "Will you at this time restore the kingdom to Israel?" the disciples ask (Acts 1:6). "The creation waits with eager longing for the revealing of the sons of God," wrote Paul to the Romans, saying also, at another point in his letter, "Besides, you know what hour it is, how it is full time now for you to wake from sleep. For the liberation is nearer to us now than when we first believed. The night is far gone; the day is at hand." (Rom. 8:18, 13:11) And to the believers in Thessalonica he had written, "This we declare to you by the word of the Lord, that we who are alive, who are left until the coming of the Lord, shall not precede those who have fallen asleep." (1 Thess. 4:15) And as perhaps the clearest expression of the pain of waiting, the author of 2 Peter (3:3 ff.) warned his readers that scoffers, as he put it, "will come in the last days, saying 'Where is the promise of his coming? For ever since the fathers fell asleep, all things continued as they were from the beginning of creation.'" And he goes on to comfort them with the sober but somewhat dampening thought that the Creator can't tell time, that a thousand years are to him the same as a day. Nevertheless, he concludes by showing no doubt that, in spite of the delay, the day of the Lord will come as a thief in the night.

These passages provide painfully clear evidence that the apostolic community found itself faced with a strange new fact for which it had not been prepared: the fact of God's delay. The messianic age, the reign of God and his annointed, was overdue. The longer the delay lasted, the harder it evidently became for the community—until the cover-up began, sometime in that dark period from which we have so few records. That was around the first centennial of the Church. But shortly, as we begin again to hear from what was by then the growing, increasingly self-confident and increasingly triumphalistic Christian movement of the second century, the agonizing seems to have died away. Every so often the fact that the age of the Messiah was an object of hope, not memory, has been rediscovered by some eccentric individuals or groups, but on the whole, the cover-up has been most successful. What had been such a problem for the early community, the inexplicable and inordinate delay in the arrival of the era which Jesus had said, and his disciples had believed, was just about to begin, seemed to become no problem at all. One might think that with the delay now having stretched out to almost nineteen and a half centuries, the pain would have become unbearable. On the contrary, the difficulty was taken in stride and so disguised as to convince most that it had never been there in the first place.

How was this fantastic sleight-of-hand accomplished? Well, in more ways than one. In fact, three different ways were used, which might be called three phases of the continuing cover-up. Phase 1 featured the mythological way of hiding the potentially embarrassing delay. We can call it mythological because it depends on setting up (quite unconsciously, of course) a mythological scenario and casting all the previous facts into this new form. With the slightest fudging of the records, Jesus comes preaching not a new era of divine righteousness and peace on earth, but another world, running parallel so to speak, to this world. All the talk about that era being invisible, as the future is always invisible, is now read as though that other world, that one up there, is invisible in principle. No longer did men and women have to long for, pray for, and struggle for a righteousness here on earth; the realm of righteousness that mattered was up there in the clouds. This world was thereby reduced to a practice-field for the great game to be played out in that ahistorical realm of eternity. As a result, it seemed as if there had been no delay at all.

This little shift having been accomplished, the way was clear to proclaim Easter as an unqualified total triumph. What it had not accomplished, including such minor details as the end of human suffering, sickness, injustice, oppression and torture, death, much of it horrible, of men, women, and children, not omitting those

slaughtered by the Romans in Jerusalem in the year 70
—all such details were simply scaled down in value in
the mythological scenario as being of only transient
concern. After all, with eternal life won, why care about
actual human life? If a righteousness of faith by grace
was available, what matter that simple human righteousness be trampled by tyranny and corruption?
Souls were being saved; what matter that their bodies
were being tortured? The more triumphalist the mythological interpretation of Easter, the more Christianity
could calmly ignore the world which it had claimed
that God so loved.

With phase 1 well launched, the cover-up proceeded
into phase 2, which may be called the institutional
phase. Having replaced the cup of cold water which
Jesus had thought so important with the cup of salvation, it was now appropriate to make the holder of that
cup into the realized promised reign of God itself. Was
liberation promised? Then enter the Church, and you
are thereby liberated. Indeed, no liberation outside the
Church! Since the kingdom was to cover the earth, the
Church set out to conquer the known world, using the
sword when the word failed. If proof was needed that
Jesus was Lord, there stood his Church, with his vicar
at its head, as the Church grew into a mighty army
before which even emperors had to bow. Could there
be any doubt that Jesus was utterly triumphant? The
triumphal Church was the living proof.

Finally, to make the case air-tight, a third phase was
developed, which we may call the individualistic phase.
In place of a longing for the Messiah to establish his
righteousness upon the whole earth, the Church began
to proclaim that each individual would go at his death
to be with the Messiah in that other invisible world. The

early Christians had thought that when we die, one by one, we fall asleep, and that when the Messiah comes, we would all be awakened and march into the new era arm in arm with those alive at the time (1 Thess 4:15–17; 1 Cor. 15:51). It was to be a revolution of un-qualifiedly social character, affecting the whole of humanity together. Now, thanks to phase 3, we don't need to worry, as did the authors of the apostolic writings, that none of this has happened yet. In this scenario it is happening all the time, one by one, and the delay simply disappears.

So the cover-up was accomplished, although we have no reason to suppose that it was done all that deliberately. Most cover-ups aren't all that deliberate. They just sort of happen, or at least get started; once started, it seems natural to go on with them. The Church's new scenario proved to be remarkably adaptable to the great pagan themes of Neo-Platonism and the mystery religions. In order to win a hearing the Church had only to spiritualize its apostolic writings and the Scriptures, and how could that be wrong? Only those awful Jews (the Church was forgetting that Jesus and all his disciples and apostles were Jews) could be interested in such worldly matters as human freedom, actual liberation on earth, and concrete lives and societies of righteousness. Turning its back on Judaism, therefore, and so upon Israel's calling to a role in God's plans for this his only creation, Christianity was left prey to the mysticism and dualism of pagan spirituality. The more it discovered that its scenario appealed to the pagan world, the more it felt sure that it now had the story right.

Christians living in America, however, need to reflect further on the fact that this new scenario would seem almost to have been designed for a much more recent development: that of the American system, and especially the patterns of thought which that system was to cultivate. We are becoming increasingly aware, we have suggested, just how mythological the American dream is, as we fittingly call our particular national nightmare. If one listens with care to the words of our highest administrators and of those we call our congressional leaders, one will hear three recurring phrases: "spiritual values," "our institutions" (sometimes "our democratic institutions"), and "the individual," made into an abstraction in such variations as "respect for the individual," "the rights of the individual," "individual liberties," and the like. When we set these abstractions of spiritual values, our institutions, and the individual, over against the hard, concrete realities of our real, economic values, of the corporations which dictate the policies of our institutions, and of the systemic reality which shapes all of our individual lives along well-established paths, we can begin to see an interesting pattern. It is almost as if Christianity had been preparing that three-phased cover-up so as to correlate precisely with the later development of American ideology; or rather, it is as if the American ideology, and this seems historically more reasonable, is to a remarkable extent shaped by the Christian cover-up, the two ending up as perfect allies in the work of hiding the reality of concrete history. How else could we expect things to have turned out, but that America must think itself the favorite of Christianity's God? (We recall Abraham Lincoln's designation of Americans as "the almost-chosen people.") And likewise, how else but that Christianity must have become more acculturated, more at ease, financially and intellectually, in the United States than anywhere else, with a prominent Protestant Evangelical and a

Catholic Jesuit priest both defending a disreputable figure in the White House to the bitter end?

Once we become aware of this fascinating symbiotic relationship between a Christianity that has denied its foundations and an American system with its abstract ideology, we can easily see that there is nothing surprising at all about the fact that Christianity, under the great cover-up, has been, is today, and is expected by the rest of the world to remain, along with America, solidly on the side of the oppressors and against the oppressed. For the condition of the oppressed is not spiritual, whereas Christianity has become spiritual. It is the lot of the oppressed to be excluded from institutions, but Christianity has been institutionalized. And the problem of the oppressed is corporate and systemic, whereas Christianity is only interested in the individual. It seems reasonable to conclude that Christianity is not likely to become a force for liberation in this world until its cover-up of God's great delay is abandoned. To do that, however, would entail pulling our heads out of those pagan, spiritualizing abstractions and planting our feet on the solid ground of the history from which we came. That in turn means to rediscover our relationship to the Jews, and to their concrete reality of flesh, history, a people, the land, and righteousness practiced in the light of Torah.

No way back to our roots has more to commend it than listening in a new way to that central proclamation of the apostles from which the Church began. What we have to attempt is a new kind of listening to what they actually had to say as witnesses of Easter, because our hearing has been impaired by a past event similar to one with which we are all familiar. When we have family quarrels, and all of us have, be it between husband and wife, father and son, mother and daughter, and all the variations on those relationships, we learn that real trouble comes when we cut each other off. It is of the essence of continuing relationships (and this is at the heart of God's covenant with Israel, a point which we need to learn again and again) that the lines of contact not be cut off. The Church's great failure was that it cut off the family quarrel with the Synagogue. Had it not done so, it could never have gotten away with the cover-up we have been considering, and had it not done so, its way back to a fresh hearing of the apostolic witness to Easter would be much easier.

Our task, then, is to win our way to a fresh hearing of the apostolic witness (made by men who were all Jews), to that which took place on the first day of the week after the feast of Passover, in what appears to have been the thirtieth year of what has come to be regarded as the common era of Jews and Gentiles of the West. To do this, we need to listen as people who have not forgotten Israel's history from its beginnings, nor its history in our day, so that we listen to these writings within and as a part of this continuing story of God's people.

The oldest extended testimony is that of Paul in his first letter to the Corinthian community, where evidently some of the group had been arguing that there was no such thing as a resurrection of the dead. Paul doesn't give us further details, so we can only guess at their position. Perhaps these were Gentiles whose idea of liberation was the tamer (we might say more rational) view that liberation was a personal, internal affair, a freeing of the spirit. Between such good Stoic views and those of a Jew like Paul lay a great gulf. No Jew could settle for such a passive, interior, individual concept of liberation. Paul's God was creator of sky and earth, fully committed to the human enterprise in all its economic, political, and social dimensions. The liberation of such a God could only be a creaturely, tangible, embodied and thoroughly social liberation. So Paul set out to argue that Easter was the definitive refutation of this personal, private and interior religion (1 Cor. 15).

He began by reminding the Corinthians (vv. 1 ff.) of his first preaching to them, which would probably have been in the year 50 C.E., and he said he passed on to them what had been passed on to him, so we have grounds for thinking we are getting close to the earliest strata of the oral tradition. That message begins with the dual affirmation that the Messiah died for our sins and was raised on the third day, each assertion followed by the phrase "in accordance with the scriptures," reflecting Paul's rabbinic training (vv. 3–4). There is no scriptural support for the idea that the Messiah would die, on behalf of our sins or otherwise, and it takes some twisting to make any biblical text about being raised up fit the idea of resurrection. But Paul and the tradition before him were certain that what God had done in the death and resurrection of Jesus was in accordance with his continuing relationship with Israel, and in that sense, it was all "in accordance with the scriptures," as we could also say of the Holocaust and the Return of the 1940s. The story is a consistent one: the righteous suffer in this age, but God is their hope and gives them signs of a liberation to come, that they may keep up the struggle.

Paul then listed a series of Jesus's appearances to three individuals, of whom Peter was the first and he himself the last, and also appearances to three groups (vv. 5–8). The risen one appeared again and again as though testing and probing the limits of his new situation of semi-liberation, or perhaps trying to make clear to the disciples that even so partial and inconclusive a victory was nevertheless real. In either case, it had the same effect that Israel had always discovered each time God acted to give a sign of what was still to come: it stirred to action and renewed hope those who saw it, and Paul, as the last witness of the event, said that it caused him to work harder than any of the others, a fact for which he claimed no credit at all (vv. 9–10).

So then, Paul argued (vv. 12ff.), if there is no resurrection, if God is not really planning a real, earthly, bodily, historical liberation of actual people in this actual world, then how come Easter? Or, in the face of the inescapable hint which Easter provides, how can you say that that real liberation does not lie ahead of us? But in fact, he goes on (vv. 20ff.), the Messiah has been raised from the dead, as the first fruits of a liberated humanity. For as in Adam, all die—that is, as Adam is the one who leads the way for us in the old age—so also in Christ shall all be made alive. If that means anything, it means that what happened on Easter is the sign, the first indication, of a liberation which God proposes for all men, and so for Judas Iscariot and Pilate as well as for Peter and Paul, for Hitler and Goering as well as for their six million victims. Freedom as a Christian goal? Yes, freedom as God's goal for the totality of his creation, going all the way to freedom from death.

But that overcoming of the last enemy, that final victory of which Easter is the ambiguous sign, lies in God's future, in what Paul and the oral tradition called "the end," (v. 24). Whether Paul was speculating about what that final goal will be like when he tried to answer the question (which may have been asked somewhat sarcastically by some of those Corinthians): "With what sort of body will the dead rise (v. 35)?" or whether he had in mind whatever it was that he saw when Jesus appeared to him, he did not say. His imagery is strange, his analogies far-fetched. How else are we to speak of matters so far removed from ordinary experience? Paul used a variety of terms for that new condition of the end, but one was that we would have bodies of glory (vv. 40–43), freed of corruption and all else that limits us in this age of oppression. With that as God's goal for us, as part of a radically new creation, Paul concluded, we can lift up our heads and work for all we are worth on the side of all that points in that direction (v. 58).

It seems clear from this sample of the witness of the apostles that the strange happening, which we call the resurrection of Jesus, was understood from the beginning as the first sign of the revolutionary new creation for which Israel longed. Paul rejoiced because the victory was about to unfold, the end was at hand, it had already broken through in Jesus as a sign of what was about to explode over the whole of humanity. In itself, then, Easter was a hint, a first glimpse of a victory about to unfold but not yet present. As the years passed, as we have seen, the delay became harder and harder to live with. Instant liberation was what Israel had always wanted, and it was what Jesus proclaimed. It was what Paul wanted too. But I think we have to digest the fact that there is something wrong here. Instant liberation may be what we all want, but it is quite evidently not what God intended, whether we like it or not. Christianity at a very early stage made a fateful move, however, toward settling the problem by transferring it out of history into a realm above. That made it possible to have instant liberation, but the price paid was heavy.

This world had to be left to itself, with liberation removed as a real possibility. "Pie in the sky when you die" may never decay, but it won't feed starving babies either. Turning its back on those that starve is the price Christianity had to pay once it decided to solve the difficulty of the delay of the messianic age by deciding that Easter was not a hint to stir us to work all the harder for liberation, but was itself the great victory opening up to us a door leading out of this world and into the higher realms of Neo-Platonism.

If we are ever going to get up the nerve to repent of that fateful move, and to turn back to picking up the hint that was given to mankind on Easter as just that, a hint of what lies ahead and for which we must work, then we shall have to face up to the way in which we have interpreted the messiahship of Jesus. The author of the Gospel according to Mark made this a turning point in his story. Peter's answer to the question of Jesus, "Who do you say that I am?" was, "You are the Messiah" (Mark 8:29). No, says Judaism. Yes, says Christianity. But what is the issue? Messiah, according to Jewish hope, has been the one whom God would send to lead his people into the new age. He would be anointed (which is what the Hebrew word *Messiah* means), that is, dedicated, commissioned by God, as the inaugurator of the age of total liberation, the agent of God's new creation. To speak of that day when the Messiah comes is the same, then, as to speak of the day when the reign of God begins.[3] What Peter said, then, reflected his conviction that the new age was breaking

[3]Or it is to speak of a messianic era that would immediately precede the final victory. For examples of the range of rabbinic ideas on this, see *A Rabbinic Anthology*, pp. 581 ff.

in, that the new creation was about to begin, and that Jesus was there in their midst to start the revolution. Evidently, so Jesus thought too, for standing in their midst, he is reported to have said that the reign of God was among them (Luke 17:21), breaking in upon them in his own person. (If one doesn't mind making Jesus self-contradictory, one can translate that grammatically as "The reign of God is within you," and thereby support phase 3 of the cover-up. But then one makes nonsense of the rest of his teaching, (e.g., Luke 17:24; Mark 13:24–27.)

Yes, say the Jews, but it didn't happen, and it hasn't happened yet. And must we not concede that they do have a point? Nineteen and a half centuries have passed and the world has become more complex, but hardly more liberated. I think we must be much clearer than we have been in speaking to Judaism and say that in the sense in which Judaism has awaited the Messiah, Jesus was not the Messiah. That having been said, however, I do not think we can leave it at that, for the very fact of our being here, Gentiles who worship Israel's God, points to the fact that Jesus was a prophet and more than a prophet. What happened with his coming forces us to say to Judaism that their conception of the Messiah has to be adjusted to whatever new thing that God does. Jesus was far from the first Jew who had to say, "You have heard it said of old, but I say to you a new thing" (*cf.* Jer. 7:4 ff.; Ezek. 12:22 ff., 18:2 ff.). The God of Israel is free in his mystery to do more than one new thing, and on this the witness of the Scriptures is clear. Again and again, Israel, Judaism and the Church have been sure that they had God's plan all figured out, only to be surprised and sometimes shocked into acknowledging the mystery of his freedom.

We are confronted in Jesus with another new thing:
a prophet and more than a prophet, a messiah before
his time, whose death and resurrection forced open a
door to the Gentile world in a quite unexpected way,
but which did not usher in the messianic age. We are
confronted in Jesus both with that new thing which did
happen, and also with the fact of what did not and still
has not happened. We have to understand him, then,
both in the apostolic witness to him, and also in that
which has happened since, as a clue to our reading of
the apostles. What has happened since can be summed
up in one word; for all that concerns the freedom for
which creation groans, what has happened is—nothing!

Nothing? Perhaps we can qualify that ever so slightly.
We find ourselves not in the time of God's victory, but
in the time of God's patience, and of this too more than
one of the apostolic writings make mention (Rom.
2:3–5; Col. 3:3–4; 2 Pet. 3:9). The Messiah, one annointed by God for this new stage in the history of Israel
and the world, came, was crucified, died and was buried. On the third day he was raised from the dead, and
then, what might have been the sound of trumpets of
victory is unexpectedly drowned out by the screech of
brakes, as God calls a halt in the further unfolding of his
purpose. And as the halt has now lasted over nineteen
centuries, one might think that God was and is trying
to say something to us. It would seem that he is saying,
no return of the Messiah, no Day of the Lord, no messianic Kingdom, until—until you get on your feet and
start to prepare the way, until you set out to walk in a
new way, in newness of life as Paul phrased it (Rom.
6:4), until you start working out your own liberation in
fear and trembling, another way that Paul put it (Phil.
2:12). In short, God is waiting for us, the Messiah is

waiting for us, waiting for us to join them in groaning and striving for the liberation of creation.

Easter and God's delay: together they tell us that to believe is to work, and thereby is dissolved the issue that split the Church in the sixteenth century, as well as part of the issue that split the Church and the Synagogue in the first century. When grace is seen as the gift of this new situation by this God, the God of Easter and of the delay, the God of this Messiah who came and returned only as a hint, not as a victory, and so for whom we wait still, then grace is what drives us to works of righteousness. Of course it is God who justifies. Who else but the Judge may pronounce the judgment of mercy? But his very mercy is designed to drive us to work, to do all within our power to work out this world's liberation with fear and trembling, knowing that it is just this God of mysterious freedom who has set us to this task. Then both sides of the sixteenth-century debate need correction and should see their differences as a quarrel within one family. When they can learn to do that with respect to Judaism, they may at the same time learn to do it with respect to each other.

The mystery of Easter and God's delay, taken together, are the revelation, the unveiling of the mystery of God's own self. Israel is where this God is known and he is adored and worshiped in Israel, in both Synagogue and Church. In the Shema and the Credo, the mystery of his freedom, his own self, is confessed. Israel confesses that it is the mystery of his freedom that he is free to qualify his own freedom by creating, really creating, and so allowing room for a world and mankind to walk freely toward the liberation which he intends.

Israel confesses this further mystery of his freedom, that he has further qualified his freedom by having from all eternity a plan and purpose for his creature, a word of liberation to this creature. That word came to Abraham as call and promise. It came also to Moses, with whom God shared his way for men and women, giving them Torah to walk by, as a light for feet stumbling toward the life of righteousness. It came again and again as a word of judgment and mercy to the prophets of Israel. This is the same plan that became flesh and blood in the man Jesus of Nazareth, annointed to voice this word of liberation: Take up your bed and walk! Go and sin no more! Lazarus, come forth!

And Israel confesses again the mystery of God's freedom in this third way, that God is free to awaken from us a response, to open our ears to hear him and to set us on fire to serve him, so working within us that we are driven to work out our own liberation, and therefore first of all the liberation of the least of our brothers and sisters, in fear and trembling.

Just this one God in the mystery of his freedom is him whom Israel confesses, Judaism in the words of the Shema: Hear, O Israel, the Lord our God is one God, and you shall love the Lord your God with all your heart, soul and might. And Christianity too in the words of the Credo: I believe in one God, Father, Son, Spirit.

In the mystery of his freedom, this God is the living God, free to call us today, in our own time, and out of the fires of the Holocaust and from the ashes of his own people. But strangest of all, he is free also and free still to open our eyes to see and our ears to hear, to hear his command to rebuild the walls of Jerusalem. As it has always been for him, he calls the Jew first, but then also the Gentile. Some of his people hear, as has also always been the case. Those Jews who have heard the voice out of Auschwitz have answered that they will do all they can that Israel may survive, that death shall not have the last word.[4] Gentiles may also respond, by standing up to walk toward and work for the liberation of his whole creation, making no peace with oppression. Since the Messiah has not yet returned, we may presume that God waits our fuller response. As of this moment, the next move appears to be ours. Such is the mystery of freedom.

[4]See Emil Fackenheim, *God's Presence in History,* New York, 1970.

EPILOGUE

I should like to close with a "rabbinic" tale, as far as I know it. There was a man who had two sons, his well-beloved first-born, and, years later, a second whom he also loved and who learned almost all he knew from his elder brother. One day the younger son said to his elder brother, "It is with us as with Jacob and Esau: it is I who have become the preferred son." They quarreled, and the younger son gathered all he could lay his hands on and took his journey into a far country. There he gave himself out as the only son of a rich man and ran up a staggering debt. The elder son, hearing of this and wishing to protect his father's good name, labored hard and suffered grievously in an attempt to lessen the indebtedness. Finally, his credit rating sinking, the younger son came to himself and resolved to return and repair the damage he had done, saying, "My father and my brother, I have sinned against heaven and before you both, and am no longer worthy to be called your son and brother. Let me become your agent to restore your fortune, your health, and your noble name throughout the world. . . ."

I have heard it said that the tale concludes with the younger son carrying out his resolution, but I cannot vouch for the authenticity of that ending.